Items should be returned to the library from which they were borrowed on or before the date stamped above, unless a renewal has been granted.

LM6.108.5

Wiltshire
COUNTY COUNCIL

BYTHESEA
ROAD

EDUCATION & LIBRARIES

TROWBRIDGE

100%
recycled paper.

Cormac McCarthy lives in El Paso, Texas. His novels *The Orchard Keeper*, *Outer Dark*, *Child of God*, *Suttree*, *Blood Meridian*, *All the Pretty Horses* and *The Crossing* are all available in Picador.

THE STONEMASON

A Play in Five Acts

CORMAC McCARTHY

PICADOR

First published 1994 by The Ecco Press, Hopewell, New Jersey

First published in Great Britain 1997 by Picador
an imprint of Macmillan Publishers Ltd
25 Eccleston Place London SW1W 9NF
and Basingstoke

Associated companies throughout the world

ISBN 0 330 35033 1

1 3 5 7 9 8 6 4 2

A CIP catalogue record for this book is available from
the British Library.

Printed and bound in Great Britain by
Mackays of Chatham plc, Chatham, Kent

THE STONEMASON

CAST OF CHARACTERS

In Order of Appearance

BEN TELFAIR
PAPAW—*his grandfather*
MAMA—*his mother*
SOLDIER—*his nephew*
BIG BEN—*his father*
CARLOTTA—*his sister*
MAVEN—*his wife*
MELISSA—*his daughter*
MRS RAYMOND—*a neighbor*
OSREAU—*a worker*
JEFFREY—*a neighbor boy*
MASON FERGUSON—*Carlotta's suitor*
GUESTS
CHILDREN
PHOTOGRAPHER
REPORTER
RELATIVES
WORKER
MINISTER
MARY WEAVER—*Big Ben's mistress*

ACT I

SCENE I

An old victorian house in the black section of Louisville Kentucky in February of 1971. The inhabitants are four generations of a black family named Telfair. It is midnight. At curtain rise there is a single light burning stage right where BEN TELFAIR *sits at a small table. He is a thirty-two year old black stonemason. Behind him and to the right is a high basement window and the soft blue light from a streetlamp. Outside in this light a softly falling snow. At far stage left is a podium or lectern at which Ben will speak his monologues throughout the play. It is important to note that the Ben we see onstage during the monologues is a double and to note that this double does not speak, but is only a figure designed to complete the scene. The purpose, as we shall see, is to give distance to the events and to place them in a completed past. The onstage double should nevertheless be as close to Ben in appearance as is practicable and the two should at all times be dressed identically. What must be kept in mind is that the performance consists of two separate presentations. One is the staged drama. The other is the monologue—or chautauqua—which Ben delivers from the podium. And while it is true that Ben at his podium is at times speaking for—or through—his silent double on stage, it is nevertheless a crucial feature of the play that there be no suggestion of communication between these worlds. In this sense it would not even be incorrect to assume that Ben is unaware of the staged drama. Above all we must resist the temptation to see the drama as something being presented by the speaker at his lectern, for to do so is to defraud the drama of its right autonomy. One could say that the play is an artifact of history to which the audience is made privy, yet if the speaker at his podium apostrophizes the figures in that history it is only as they reside in his memory. It is this which dictates the use of the podium. It locates Ben in a separate space and isolates that space from the world of the drama on stage. The speaker has an agenda which centers upon his own exoneration, his own salvation. The events which unfold upon the stage will not at all times support him. The audience may perhaps be also a jury. And now we can begin. As the mathematician Gauss said to his contemporaries: Go forward and faith will come to you. The podium is lit. Ben comes forward to take his place there. As he begins to speak, his double seated at the table onstage begins to write.*

BEN I always wanted to be like him. Even as a child. I was twelve when my grandmother died and then he came to this house and I began to see him every day and my mother would laugh at me because I had even begun to walk like him. And he was eighty-five years old.

Lights come on in the kitchen of the house at stage center. Ben looks up from his desk toward the kitchen—which is upstairs. The kitchen represents the principal set of the play. It is an oldfashioned kitchen from the early 1900's with a wainscotting of narrow tongue-and-groove boards, a long kitchen table with chairs, a range, a sink, a refrigerator. An oldfashioned woodburning stove. At the rear are two doors, one leading outside and the other giving onto the bedroom of Ben's grandfather, PAPAW. *This door now opens and Papaw comes into the kitchen.*

He is 101 years old, small and wiry and fit. He goes to the sink and fills the kettle and puts it on the stove and goes to the woodstove and pokes up the fire.

BEN He's come into the kitchen to fix his tea. Sometimes I go up and we have tea together. Three oclock in the morning. Nothing surprises him. He has no schedule. Sometimes we talk and sometimes not. Sometimes we talk straight through till breakfast and Mama comes down and she looks at us but she doesnt say anything. He does not need much sleep and I am like him in this also.

Papaw comes back to the stove and fixes his tea and takes it to the table and sits down. On the table is an old leatherbound bible.

BEN He was an old man before I was born and I have loved him all my life and love him now.

Papaw sips his tea and takes out his little wireframed glasses and puts them on and opens the bible.

BEN People believe that the stonemasons of his time were all like him but that was never so. Anything excellent is always rare. He's been a stonemason for ninety years, starting as a boy, mixing the old lime mortar with a hoe, fitting spalls. He has thought deeply about his trade and in this he's much out of the ordinary. His entire life's work lies in five counties in this state and two across the river in Indiana. I've spent a lot of time looking at it. Maybe ten percent survives. I can look at a wall or the foundation of a barn and tell his work from the work of other masons even in the same structure. If we're out in the truck and I point out his work to him he merely nods. The work he's done is no monument. The stonework out there at night in the snow and the man who laid that stone are each a form of each and forever joined. For I believe that to be so. But the monument is upstairs. Having his tea.

Ben sits back in his chair and looks out the high window. Sound of a car going up the street in the muffled snow, chains clinking. He bends to his desk again.

BEN For the past two years he's been helping me build my house. Or rebuild it. It's the house that he grew up in. We go out there on week-ends.

The kitchen and basement lights dim to black.

BEN Sometimes Maven and Melissa come and we have a picnic. Sometimes Mama too. The house is stone and it is laid up in the old style with lime mortar. It was built long before the introduction of portland cement made it possible to build with stone and yet know nothing of masonry.

Lights come on downstage right revealing the exterior of the two storey stone farmhouse partly in ruins. At the front is a low partial wall of actual stone and here Ben and Papaw are at work together laying stone, chipping it with hammer and chisel, passing their trowels over the work and setting the stone in place.

BEN For true masonry is not held together by cement but by gravity. That is to say, by the warp of the world. By the stuff of creation itself. The keystone that locks the arch is pressed in place by the thumb of God. When the weather is good we gather the stone ourselves out of the fields. What he likes best is what I like. To take the stone out of the ground and dress it and put it in place. We split the stones out along their seams. The chisels clink. The black earth smells good. He talks to me about stone in a different way from my father. Always as a thing of consequence. As if the mason were a custodian of sorts. He speaks of sap in the stone. And fire. Of course he's right. You can smell it in the broken rock. He always watched my eyes to see if I understood. Or to see if I cared. I cared very much. I do now. According to the gospel of the true mason God has laid the stones in the earth for men to use and he has laid them in their bedding planes to show the mason how his own work must go. A wall is made the same way the world is made. A house, a temple. This gospel must accommodate every inquiry. The structure of the world is such as to favor the prosperity of men. Without this belief nothing is possible. What we are at arms against are those philosophies that claim the fortuitous in mens' inventions. For we invent nothing but what God has put to hand.

The lights illuminating the stone house and the workers have dimmed to black.

BEN Were it not for him I'd have become a teacher. I nearly did. I nearly did.

The lights come up at the basement desk and window. In the kitchen. Ben sits at his desk. Papaw sits at the kitchen table reading his bible.

BEN He never suggested that it would not be a good trade for me. He even encouraged me, although I knew that when I told him I was studying psychology he had little notion of what that meant. Fair enough. Psychology has little notion of what he means. Never did he smile at my pretensions. It was only when I came home after my first year of graduate school that I realized my grandfather knew things that other people did not and I began to clear my head of some of the debris that had accumulated there and I did not go back to school that fall and I did not go back that winter and by then I had already begun to learn the trade that anyone would have said I already knew since I'd worked at it for ten years and paid for my schooling with it. A trade at which I thought myself a master and of which I stood in darkest ignorance. And as I came to know him . . . As I came to know him . . . Oh I could hardly believe my good fortune. I swore then I'd cleave to that old man like a bride. I swore he'd take nothing to his grave.

SCENE II

Early the following morning. The lights are on in the kitchen and outside it is just graying with daylight. Papaw is sitting in his chair by the stove as Ben enters.

BEN Morning Papaw. [Pap-paw]
PAPAW Mornin Ben. Mornin.

Ben goes to the window and looks out at the yard. There is a small dog sleeping by the stove and it looks up.

BEN What do you think?
PAPAW Well. Be a mite slick out I expect.

MAMA, *Ben's mother enters the kitchen. A bustling and somewhat harriedlooking woman in her fifties. She eyes them suspiciously and goes on to the stove and gets the coffee percolator and goes to the sink with it.*

BEN You want to go out to the farm?
MAMA (*Speaking loudly over the sound of the faucet*) He aint goin nowhere with you in this.

Ben smiles at his grandfather. Mama turns off the faucet and takes the percolator to the stove.

MAMA So dont you even start.

PAPAW You reckon we get out there?

MAMA Papaw dont you pay no attention to him he aint got no sense.

She puts coffee in the percolator and she takes down a large black skillet and spoons lard into it.

SOLDIER *enters the kitchen. He is Ben's sister's son, aged fifteen.*

MAMA You just the man I want to see. Get them plates and set the table.

SOLDIER I just come in to see if they's any school today.

MAMA No, you just come in to set the table.

Soldier drags himself to the cupboard and takes down the plates.

MAMA And when you get done with that holler upstairs at Big Ben.

PAPAW Everthing be covered up.

MAMA Benny I done told you all now.

PAPAW Too cold to mix mud and that's for sure.

BEN I'm not going to do any work out there. I'm just going to haul a load of stone out.

MAMA You aint takin him noplace in Old Blue. That thing aint got no heater in it.

There are heavy footsteps on the stairs overhead. BIG BEN, *Ben's father, enters the kitchen. He is wearing slippers and a pair of tan gabardine slacks with suspenders over a longsleeved winter undershirt. He has on three or four very expensive rings that he wears when not working. He weighs over two hundred and fifty pounds and he goes to the stove with the rolling gait of heavy people and takes his cup and pours coffee from the percolator.*

MAMA That aint done perkin.

He continues to pour and then takes up his cup and takes his watch out of his pocket although there is an electric clock on the stove and another clock on the wall. He puts the watch back in his pocket and shuffles back across the kitchen and out the door.

BEN *(To Papaw)* You want some coffee?
PAPAW Might have just a little coffee this mornin.

Ben goes to the stove and takes two cups and pours coffee. Mama is busy cooking at the stove. In the front room offstage the door slams.

BIG BEN *(Offstage)* Who got the paper?
MAMA Aint nobody got the paper. He aint run yet.

Ben takes the cups to the woodstove and gives one to his grandfather. Mama takes a platter of sausage to the table.

MAMA You all come on now.

Ben and Papaw start towards the table. Soldier reaches and takes a patty of sausage from the platter and is on the way to his mouth with it when she intercepts it and puts it back on the platter and slaps him on the back of the head with her open hand and sets the platter down all in one motion as if she'd had practice at it.

MAMA Get the chair boy, get the chair. You all come on now. Carlotta! Benny where's Maven? I aint cookin no two breakfasts.

Ben's sister CARLOTTA enters on her high heels dressed for work. Soldier brings the extra chair from its place against the wall and Ben goes to the door and calls downstairs for Maven. Big Ben appears and takes his place at the head of the table and begins to help his plate to eggs. Ben comes to the table and Mama brings the percolator from the stove and sets it on the table.

MAMA Carlotta, did you want to say grace?

CARLOTTA Bless O Lord this food to our nourishment and us to thy service. Amen.

FAMILY Amen.

BIG BEN Where's Maven?

Ben pushes his chair back and rises.

MAMA Set still. Soldier you run downstairs and see if she comin to breakfast this mornin.

BEN I'll go.

MAMA Maybe she sick.

SOLDIER What she got?

MAMA Just eat, boy.

Ben exits. The family continues to eat, to pass plates. A radio on the sideboard is giving local news, the volume comes up slowly.

CARLOTTA What do they say about school?

SOLDIER Aint said nothin yet that I heard.

MAMA Well you better be for findin out.

SOLDIER Well let me call Jeffrey.

MAMA How he supposed to know?

SOLDIER Cause he the man that knows, that's how.

CARLOTTA Dont smartmouth your grandmama.

SOLDIER Aint smartmouthin nobody. She ast me and I told her.

CARLOTTA And dont smartmouth me either. And you better stay away from that boy. If he's not on his way to the penitentiary there's no use in having one.

SOLDIER Shoot.

Big Ben casts a suspicious glance at Soldier. Soldier crams a last forkful of food into his mouth and rises from the table. He makes his way around the table and goes to the telephone on the sideboard and dials a number. He stands with his back to the table and puts his thumb down on the receiver. He talks a little too loud. The family continues to eat.

BIG BEN Pass the preserves yonder, Carlotta.

SOLDIER Yeah. Soldier. You heard anything bout school? Mm hm. Aint goin be none. Called your mama? Yeah. On the radio too? Naw we didnt hear it. Bout half a hour ago?

The telephone rings. Soldier freezes. The family at the table stop eating and look at Soldier. The telephone rings again. Carlotta and Mama rise at the same moment. Soldier holds the telephone away from his ear and looks at it and puts it to his ear again.

SOLDIER Hello? Hello?

Ben enters the kitchen. The phone rings again. Carlotta reaches Soldier first.

MAMA Fool. If I dont put a knot on your head.

SOLDIER There's somethin wrong with this phone.

Carlotta snatches the phone from him and raps him on the top of the head with it.

SOLDIER Ow!

CARLOTTA (*Putting the receiver to her ear*) Hello. Yes. Hi Jenny.

Soldier goes wide around Mama, who is taking her place at the table again. He is holding the top of his head.

SOLDIER Shit.

BIG BEN What did you say?

Soldier mutters something that no one can hear. Big Ben reaches downtable and takes a swipe at him. Soldier ducks and falls backward and the chair goes to the floor. Big Ben stands up to deal with him further and Mama stands up and takes Big Ben by the arm.

MAMA Dont hit him on the ear you'll make him deaf like they done Edison in the movie

Across the table Papaw is eating peaceably.

CARLOTTA *(Holding one hand over the receiver)* Mama make them quit.

Ben shakes his head and goes back out. Soldier gets up and rights the chair and stands there and Big Ben subsides and Mama sits back down and Ben comes back into the room with the paper and gives it to his father who glares up at him and takes it. Ben sits at the table and helps his plate to eggs and sausage and begins to eat.

MAMA *(To Soldier)* You set down over there. You aint excused. Benny is she goin to school today?

BEN Yes. She says she is.

MAMA You ask her if she looked outside?

BEN Yep.

MAMA She sick?

BEN *(Smiling)* She's sick. She's looked outside. She's going to school.

MAMA Why dont you take her a cup of coffee down there?

BEN I offered to but she said she didnt want any. *(To Big Ben)* I want to use your truck today.

BIG BEN *(Reading the paper)* Where you goin?

BEN Haul a load of rock out to the farm.

BIG BEN Dont call on me when you get stuck.

BEN I wont.

MAMA That thing aint got no heater in it and it aint got no floorboard.

Big Ben does not look up from his paper. He takes a sip of coffee and continues to read.

BIG BEN You better see if they any sand in the bed. I dont know where you get any at today.

MAMA You hear that? Twenty-two degrees.

Ben finishes his breakfast and wipes his mouth and pushes back his chair and rises and takes his plate to the sink and then goes to the door.

BEN Soldier.

SOLDIER What.

BEN Come out here a minute.

SOLDIER What for?

BEN Just come out here.

SOLDIER I aint excused.

BEN You're excused.

Soldier gets up wearily and follows Ben out of the kitchen. They come to stage left where a light illuminates a white sofa and a white chair and a coffee table.

BEN Sit down.

SOLDIER I aint tired.

BEN Just sit down.

Soldier sits wearily in the sofa and throws his arm across the back of it. Ben sits on the arm of the sofa.

BEN What do you want to do that stuff for?

SOLDIER What stuff?

BEN That telephone business. Trying to get out of school.

SOLDIER Maybe I dont want to go today.

BEN You dont want to go any day. That's not the point. You dont have a choice.

SOLDIER You aint my daddy.

BEN Is there somebody leaning on you at school?

Soldier drums his fingers on the back of the sofa in a bored fashion.

BEN Is there?

SOLDIER They aint nobody at that school that I'm scared of.

BEN What happened to your eye the other day?

SOLDIER What other day?

BEN Last week. Week and a half ago.

SOLDIER I done that playin basketball.

BEN Where were you playing basketball? You quit the team.

SOLDIER You think they aint nobody play basketball cept what's on the team?

BEN Why did you quit?

SOLDIER I dont need the aggravation.

BEN Was it because you didnt make the A team? You would of made it next year.

SOLDIER I dont need to play on no B team.

BEN Everybody starts on the B team. Dont they?

SOLDIER Not everbody.

BEN But most.

SOLDIER That's them, this is me.

Ben studies him. He shakes his head.

BEN Your mother's right you know. You're going to get in trouble running around with that bunch of trash.

SOLDIER It aint nothin to you.

BEN Yes it is.

Ben studies him.

BEN You want to work for me Saturday?

SOLDIER I got other business to tend to.

BEN All right. You want to go out and start the truck?

SOLDIER Where's the keys at?

BEN They're in it.

Soldier gets up and goes back into the kitchen and out the back door. Ben watches him go, then gets up and exits offstage. We hear him go down the steps. In the kitchen Mama is clearing the table. Papaw gets up and goes to his room.

BEN *(Offstage)* Babe, I'm gone.
   Is Melissa awake?
   Are you okay?
   All right.
   I love you.

Ben returns to the living room and enters the kitchen. Soldier comes in the back door stomping the snow off his shoes. Ben goes to the back door and takes his coat down off a peg. He looks outside. Papaw is dressed in his coat and gloves and is standing by the woodstove holding his hat.

BEN Soldier.

SOLDIER What.

BEN I thought you were going to start the truck.

SOLDIER Caint start it without no keys.

BEN The keys are in it.

SOLDIER No they aint.

BIG BEN *(Without looking up from his paper)* The keys is in it.

SOLDIER *(Looking from Ben to Big Ben and back again)* What truck you talkin bout?

Ben buttons up his coat and pulls his gloves out of his coat pocket and puts on his hat.

SOLDIER I thought you meant the pickup.

BEN You sat right there and heard us talk about Grandad's truck.

SOLDIER You said truck I thought you meant your truck.

BEN *(To his grandfather)* You ready?

Papaw claps his gloved hands together. Ben gets the thermos of coffee off the sideboard that his mother has put there and returns to the door. The dog looks after him.

BIG BEN You better get you some sand.

MAMA Dont you keep him out in this all day. You hear?

Ben opens the door.

MAMA And let Bossy out.

BEN *(To the dog)* Let's go.

The dog looks at him.

BEN Let's go, I said.

The dog climbs slowly out of the box and goes to the door and looks out.

BEN Hit it.

The dog goes out. Ben and Papaw turn up their collars and pull on their caps and let down the earflaps. Ben watches the dog out in the snow.

BEN Mama what are you going to do about this dog?

MAMA Aint nothin wrong with that dog.

BEN He raises his leg to take a pee and then falls over in it.

MAMA You dont need to be worryin bout that dog. That dog's just fine.

SCENE III

The exterior of the old stone farmhouse. Ben and Papaw bring stones from offstage and pile them among the stones in front of the house. The light comes on at the podium and Ben speaks from there.

BEN To get stone for the house we also pull down old walls that are about to be bulldozed. Often we are given the stone just to haul it away. My grandfather says that you might learn how a watch is made by taking one apart or you might even be able to learn how to build a house by tearing one down. But tearing down stonework tells you nothing. The old masons would quit work if you stopped to watch them, but I dont think you could learn by watching. You couldnt learn it out of a book if there were any and there are not. Not one. We were taught. Generation by generation. For ten thousand years. Now in the memory of a single man it's been set aside as if it never existed. As if it had no value at all. He knows this and yet it seems not to bother him.

Maven is right to be jealous of him. I know that he's going to die and I despise every hour not spent in his company.

The podium light dims to black. At the house Ben goes offstage to bring a stone from the truck. The old man pauses to relight his pipe.

PAPAW I didnt see no schoolbusses out.

BEN *(Returning with a stone)* Soldier was probably trying to lay out of a school that wasnt going to run anyway. I dont know what to do about him.

PAPAW *(Sucking at his pipe and throwing the match aside)* Well. They was a boy killed at that school. Maybe he shows pretty good sense.

BEN Maybe you're right. I knew that school was just a drug exchange center so I dont know why I should be surprised now that the murders have started. I know he's making Carlotta crazy.

PAPAW Well, the boy's daddy aint around.

BEN I think it's his daddy that's most of his problem now.

PAPAW Well. Landry aint much shakes. But it take a pretty sorry daddy to be worse than no daddy at all.

BEN I take it you dont rate him that sorry.

PAPAW A man that will work they's always hope for him. He can always change his ways.

BEN Well, he does work. What about a man that wont work?

PAPAW *(Shaking his head)* I dont believe they's nothin you can do for him. If they is I never saw it. *(He looks offstage)* That's the last one aint it?

BEN That's the last one. You want some tea?

PAPAW Well that would be all right. Too early to eat dinner.

Ben exits briefly offstage. Sound of the truckdoor opening and slamming and he returns with the thermos and cups and they sit down on the stones and Ben pours the tea.

BEN So tell me what happened about the man's house.

PAPAW Oh well. They done had it made up to go out there. They wasnt no use to consult with me.

BEN Is that what they call a crowbar lien?

PAPAW Well. I've heard it called that.

BEN But they did it anyway.

PAPAW Oh yes. They went out there and pulled it down. They had some big bars and they pried the stones out of the lower courses till it give way. They was lucky it didnt fall on em.

BEN Did you think they were wrong?

PAPAW I thought the man ought to of paid us what he owed us. Tearin it down didnt get nobody paid though. It didnt benefit nobody.

BEN Maybe it made them feel better.

PAPAW Maybe. I expect it depend on how you feel in the first place. Stonework aint like somethin you sell to a man and he dont pay you you can take it back. Even a house, you could tear it down and get the lumber. Get the brick. But the mason fits the stones for the place where they're to go and that's where they're at. They aint nothin to take back. You just has to destroy it. You destroy you own work you aint got much use for it to start with, paid or not paid.

BEN Might it not keep somebody else from not paying you?

PAPAW It might. It might keep some from hirin you too. They's lots of work in this world that aint never paid for. But the accounts gets balanced anyway. In the long run. A man that contracts for work and then dont pay for it, the world will reckon with him fore it's out. With the worker too. You live long enough and you'll see it. They's a ledger kept that the pages dont never get old nor crumbly nor the ink dont never fade. If it dont balance then they aint no right in this world and if they aint then where did I hear of it at? Where did you? Only way it wont is you start retribution on you own. You start retribution on you own you'll be on you own. That man up there aint goin to help you. Aint no use even to ask.

BEN Is that why you wouldnt go out there with them?

PAPAW No. The reason I wouldnt go out there was just a plain everday reason. No man can lay stone and be thinkin bout whether he goin to have to tear it back down again. Aint no use to get in no such habits as that. You

know that man up there aint goin to let nothin stand forever noway. Not in this world he aint. And it's against
that judgment that you got to lay stone. If you goin to lay
it at all.

BEN So who owns the stonework that's not paid for?

PAPAW Well, under the law you can get a lien on the work.
You can claim it, but you caint take possession of it. The
man you built it for, he can take possession of it, but he
caint claim it. The law dont have no answer. Where men
dont have right intentions the law caint supply em. You
just at a dead end.

BEN Then no one owns the work?

PAPAW The man's labor that did the work is in the work.
You caint make it go away. Even if it's paid for it's still
there. If ownership lies in the benefit to a man then the
mason owns all the work he does in this world and you
caint put that claim aside nor quit it and it dont make no
difference whose name is on the paper.

SCENE IV

The basement. Ben at his small table. The light comes on at the
podium.

BEN Whose work is it? I know that there are stones in
that house that his uncle Selman laid up. There's no

stone for Selman. He's buried behind the house. Somewhere on the hill. My grandfather's views must incorporate the life of Selman. All Selmans. These views appear to be some labor theory of value. But there's a further agenda. Because the world is made of stone the mason is prey to a great conceit and to whatever extent the look and the shape of the world is the work of the mason then that work exists outside of the claims of workers and landholders alike. Reading Marx in my last year of school only sent me to Hegel and there I found his paradigm of servant and master in which the master comes to suffer the inner impoverishment of the idle while the servant by his labors grows daily in skill and wisdom.

The house was built in 1836 and that date is cut into the lintel stone over the front door. The Telfairs black and white came here from South Carolina in the 1820's. His father and mother were slaves as was his brother Harris, born 1861, and his sister Emmanuelle, born Christmas day of 1862. Seven days before the signing of the Emancipation Proclamation. The stone sills of the cabin where he was born are still there behind the house.

I can remember the house when it had a roof on it. We'd take visiting relatives out there on Sundays when I was a child. There were black people living in it then but

I dont know what their name was. I bought the place in 1966, the house and forty-two acres in three separate parcels, and I gave him the deed at his one hundredth birthday party four years later. He looked at it for a long time. Nobody knew what it was that he was looking at. It got more and more quiet and finally Carlotta said: "What is it, Papaw?" and he had tears in his eyes and he just handed it to her and looked away.

He had me promise not to disturb the pale renters interred on our farm but I had no intention to do so. He says that for himself we can just throw him out in a sinkhole when he quits this world. But he'll be buried with his ancestors black and white in full possession of the earth whereunder he lies. It balances out, he says. Yes. The arc of the moral universe is indeed long but it does bend toward justice. At the root of all this of course is the trade. As he always calls it. His craft is the oldest there is. Among man's gifts it is older than fire and in the end he is the final steward, the final custodian. When the last gimcrack has swallowed up its last pale creator he will be out there, prefering the sun, trying the temper of his trowel. Placing stone on stone in accordance with the laws of God. The trade was all they had, the old masons. They understood it both in its utility and in its secret nature. We couldnt read nor write, he says. But it was not in any book. We kept it close to our hearts. We kept it close to our hearts and it was like a power and we knew it would not fail us. We knew that it was a thing that if we had it they could not take it from us and it would stand by us and not fail us. Not ever fail us.

CURTAIN

ACT II

SCENE I

Late morning in the kitchen. Ben is standing with a cup of coffee looking out the window. The breakfast dishes are on the sideboard and there is still a plate of biscuits and other things on the kitchen table. Big Ben enters. He is dressed in a doublebreasted creamcolored suit with a gabardine shirt the open collar of which is worn folded down outside the suit lapels. He carries a camelhair overcoat over his arm and a hat in his hand. Soldier comes in from outside stamping the snow from his shoes.

BIG BEN You get the rearview mirror?
SOLDIER Done got it all.

Big Ben rummages in his pocket and comes up with a quarter and doles it out to Soldier and then shrugs himself into his coat and buttons it and turns up the collar and puts on his hat and goes out.

SOLDIER I bet he tips better'n that away from the house.

BEN I bet he does too.

SOLDIER (*Looking out the window as the car pulls away*) Big Cadillac man.

BEN He worked for it.

SOLDIER What he think I goin to do with a quarter?

BEN Get in half the trouble you would if he gave you fifty cents.

SOLDIER (*Turning away from the window*) Shit.

Ben looks after him as he crosses the kitchen and exits. He looks out the window and shakes his head. Ben's wife MAVEN *enters the kitchen. She is dressed in jeans and a sweater. Ben turns and looks at her and smiles.*

MAVEN Hi.

She goes to the sink and begins to wash the dishes.

BEN Babe can you still get in those jeans?

MAVEN These are Carlotta's.

BEN Is she bigger than you?

MAVEN Yes, smartie. She's bigger than me.

BEN I dont guess Mama has any jeans does she?

MAVEN Why dont you bring your head over here where I can drub it.

BEN *(Smiling)* Drub?
MAVEN Drub.

Ben smiles and shakes his head. He drains his cup and brings it to the sink and sets it down and kisses Maven.

MAVEN What are your plans today, Hotshot?
BEN Work on the house.
MAVEN How's it coming?
BEN Why dont you come out and see?
MAVEN I've got a doctor's appointment at eleven.
BEN You could come out this afternoon.
MAVEN Will you build a fire in the fireplace?
BEN The mortar's still too wet.

Maven shakes her head.

MAVEN No deal.
BEN I could build one outside.
MAVEN Not the same thing. Are you taking Papaw with you?
BEN Yep.

She looks past him to Papaw's door.

MAVEN Ben dont you think he's a little old to be out in the freezing cold doing stonework?

BEN Well, I think he's old enough to say for himself.

MAVEN What if he died out there?

BEN Maybe he'd prefer it.

MAVEN Your mother would never forgive you.

BEN I know. I've thought about that. It's just a chance I'll have to take.

MAVEN She thinks you dont take care of him. *I* think you dont take care of him.

BEN I know. He's tougher than you think. Babe I wouldnt take him out there if it didnt mean a lot to him. That's his house. He wants to see it done. He wants to do it. He sees it as some kind of final evidence of justice in the world. For him it's like the workings of Providence.

MAVEN Has he ever said that?

BEN *(Smiling)* No.

MAVEN Do you think that?

BEN I dont know. Maybe. I think I'd like to.

MAVEN Soldier has his version too. What is it he says? What goes around comes around?

BEN I think what Soldier has in mind is revenge.

MAVEN Mm hm.

BEN *(Smiling)* Is that what justice is? Revenge?

MAVEN Probably it is for those being treated unjustly.

BEN But the rain falls on the just and the unjust.

MAVEN The rain falls upon the just
        And also on the unjust fellas

But mostly it falls upon the just
Cause the unjust have the just's umbrellas

BEN *(Smiling)* Is that what you learned in school?

MAVEN That's what I learned at my mammy's knee.

BEN Do they talk about justice in your classes or just about the law?

MAVEN Mostly the law. It's a pretty pragmatic business. I think that was an older generation that discussed the philosophy of law.

BEN Probably. Papaw was talking about the law yesterday. He says that law can only work in a just society.

MAVEN He said *that?*

BEN *(Smiling)* Well, more or less. It's what he meant anyway.

MAVEN You think his opinions are valuable because he's worked all his life. Isnt that a pretty romantic notion?

BEN Yes. It's also true. You cant separate wisdom from the common experience and the common experience is just what the worker has in great plenty.

MAVEN Then why arent more workers wise?

BEN I guess for the same reason that more college professors arent wise. Thinking's rare among all classes. But a laborer who thinks, well, his thought seems more likely to be tempered with humanity. He's more inclined to tolerance. He knows that what is valuable in life is life.

MAVEN And the professor?

BEN I think he's more apt to just be dangerous. Marx never worked a day in his life.

MAVEN Sounds a little neat to me.

BEN I dont have a theory about it. I think most people feel that books are dangerous and they're probably right.

MAVEN I'll bear that in mind.

BEN *(Smiling)* I dont think it's a problem for you. You've got a pretty good anchoring in reality anyway. One downstairs and one in here.

He puts his hand on her stomach.

MAVEN You've got a pretty romantic notion about motherhood too.

BEN I hope so.

MAVEN You're a fairly strange person. I knew that when I married you. Have you become more strange or were you hiding the worst from me?

BEN I dont hide anything from you.

She puts the last of the dishes in the drainer and wipes her hands on a towel.

MAVEN I've got to get ready.

BEN Is Melissa awake?

Maven puts her arm around Ben and kisses him.

MAVEN Yes. She's playing. *Playing*, Ben.

BEN *(Smiling)* I know how to play.

MAVEN How many block did you lay yesterday on your father's new job?

BEN It's my new job too.

MAVEN How many.

BEN Why?

MAVEN I heard you put on quite a performance.

BEN I was just working.

MAVEN You had a gallery all afternoon.

BEN Well, people dont have much to do.

MAVEN How many.

BEN Seven hundred and something.

MAVEN Seven hundred and what.

BEN Seven hundred and eighty-two.

She shakes her head.

BEN Do you want to know what that comes to in dollars?

MAVEN That's not why I asked, Ben.

BEN I know. It's mindless work. It's as easy to do fast as it is slow.

MAVEN That's not just working fast.

BEN Well. It makes it more interesting.

MAVEN Then you go out to the farm and work till eight. That's a thirteen hour day. Besides stonework that you and Papaw do on the side.

BEN I dont know any other way to do it.

MAVEN How soon are you leaving?

BEN Just a few minutes.

She kisses him again.

MAVEN Bye.

BEN I'll see you tonight.

MAVEN Look after him, Ben.

BEN You know I look after him.

MAVEN I know. Look after him anyway.

She exits.

SCENE II

The kitchen, evening. It is dark out. The supper dishes are still on the table and Mama and Carlotta are sitting at the table and MELISSA *is in a highchair. Carlotta is smoking a cigarette. Ben is standing in the kitchen dressed in a sportcoat and tie and he has his coat over his arm. Sound of steps on the basement stairs. Maven enters. She is dressed for the evening and has on her coat.*

MAMA Be slick out there, Benny. You be careful.

Maven comes to the table and kisses Mama on the cheek.

MAVEN Night Mama. Thank you.

She kisses Melissa.

MAVEN Night Punkin.

Ben is putting on his coat. Maven buttons her coat up.

BEN You ready?
MAMA What time you all be back?
BEN About daylight.
MAMA *(Laughing)* Yeah, daylight.
MAVEN We'll be back about eleven or eleven thirty.

She takes Ben's arm and they go out. Mama gets up and begins to clear away the dishes. Outside the truck doors slam and the motor starts and the truck pulls away. The lights sweep past the kitchen window. Carlotta stubs out her cigarette. Mama screws up her nose.

MAMA Shoo, girl. I dont see how you can puff on them nasty things. I'd about as soon commit fornication.
CARLOTTA So would I.

Mama has started away from the table and she turns and gives Carlotta a vicious look. Carlotta holds her hands palm up.

CARLOTTA It's a joke, Mama. A joke.

MAMA Joke? Mmph. Aint nothin to be jokin about.

CARLOTTA Well you're the one that said it, Mama.

MAMA Well it wasnt said for no joke.

She goes on to the sink. Carlotta shakes her head, smiling. Mama returns and makes a fuss over Melissa.

CARLOTTA You've got her spoiled completely rotten.

MAMA Good thing they somebody here to spoil her.

CARLOTTA You think Maven ought to be here more?

MAMA She come to me fore she will to her own mama.

CARLOTTA Well it's just temporary.

MAMA Honey life's just temporary. Besides she got two more long years in that school. And then what she goin to do? I heard of negro lawyers and I heard of women lawyers but I sure aint never heard of no negro woman lawyer. Not in Louisville Kentucky I aint.

CARLOTTA Times change, Mama.

MAMA Amen, sister, Amen. You said a mouthful when you said that. *(She sits heavily at the table).* Aint her nor Ben neither one in this house no longer'n what it takes to sleep and eat breakfast. Tell me about spoilin this child and her not much better than a orphan?

CARLOTTA Well Mama, I'd be ashamed.

MAMA Well it's the truth. What's the truth, you might as well tell it.

CARLOTTA Well I'd be afraid to start back to school. You'd be badmouthing me too.

MAMA Aint nobody badmouthin nobody. She's a sweet girl. Couldnt ask for no better hardly. She just got a lot of high tone ideas, that's all. Life'll smack a few of em out of her fore it gets done with her. Besides, Benny's the one ought to be the lawyer. He'd be a dandy too. Smart as he is.

CARLOTTA Well I declare, Mama. I dont believe I'm hearing this. You're jealous of her on Ben's part.

MAMA Aint done no such a thing. Just statin the facts, that's all.

CARLOTTA Well in any case she's here more than Ben, that's for sure.

MAMA She supposed to be.

CARLOTTA If you count the work he contracts with Papaw and the work he does out at his farm he's working three jobs. I dont see how she got pregnant the first time let alone twice.

MAMA Girl you got a mouth on you, you know that?

CARLOTTA There's nothing wrong with saying that.

MAMA Hmph.

CARLOTTA You think men are born with rights that women dont have. That they can come and go like migratory birds and it's perfectly natural . . .

MAMA It is natural. Tryin to change nature. Women has babies. You caint get around that. That's the plan the good Lord laid down and you wont change it. You can make up you own plan if you want to, and you can read it in ruin.

CARLOTTA Well, it wasnt the good Lord's plan that I ever heard of for men to be gone all hours of the day and night.

MAMA You watch yourself girl. You hear? You just watch yourself.

CARLOTTA That's what it's about.

MAMA I aint goin to tell you again.

CARLOTTA I'll tell you what you told me. The truth's the truth.

Mama gets up from the table and busies herself at the sideboard.

CARLOTTA You're right. It's none of my business.

Mama has come back to the table and is picking up Melissa.

MAMA Honey you ready to put on your jammies? You ready to go night night?

SCENE III

The kitchen, Sunday morning. The family are coming in from outside, returning from church. They disperse through the kitchen and exit, steps on the stairs both up and down, leaving Papaw and Ben in the kitchen. Ben is putting the kettle on. Papaw has taken off his overcoat and hat and laid the coat across the back of a kitchen chair. He has on an old fashioned dark suit, white shirt with tie, hightop black kid dress shoes. He sits at the kitchen table and puts his hat on the table. Ben is fixing tea.

BEN Papaw what did you think of the new minister?

PAPAW Well I liked him just fine. Liked him just fine. I didnt catch his name.

BEN Erickson. His name is Erickson.

PAPAW Erickson. I worked one time for a man named Erickson. He sure wasnt no minister.

BEN *(Smiling)* I thought you might think he was a bit young for the job.

PAPAW Well he is young. But he seemed to have good sense. Bein old dont shelter people from ignorance. Ought to, but it dont.

Ben pours the cups and brings them to the table.

PAPAW Thank you Benny. Thank you.

A lot of the old time preachers used to preach all kinds of foolishness. Or it was to my ears. I heard any number of times how when colored folks got to heaven they'd be white. Well that dont make no more sense than a goose wearin gaiters. God didnt make the colored man colored just to see how he'd look. There aint nothin triflin about God. He made everbody the color He wanted em to be and He meant for em to stay that way. And if that suits Him its got to suit me too, else I's just a damn fool.

BEN Did you always feel that way?

PAPAW I think so. I know some coloreds dont, but I always did. It was the way I was raised.

BEN Do you think it was easier growing up black back then?

PAPAW Many ways it was. Course in many ways it was easier dont matter what color you was. We lived out at the farm and we didnt have a whole lot of experience of the world. Our families, Telfair families, colored and white, we'd been together over a hundred year and we didnt encounter all that much meanness. They was good people and so was we. The first time I ever understood that the white man . . . I was six year old and they was a circus show come to Louisville and Harris, he's the oldest, he made it up for all of us to go and he got extra work for everbody and we saved them pennies, saved them pennies. I think it costed a dime to get in but we raised it. And he carried us all over there, him and Aaron and Charles and me and sister Emmanuelle she come too. We got over there and Harris had heard about the monkeys and he wanted to see em awful bad and we tried to locate where they was at and after awhile he went up to this white man was sellin lemonade, soda pop, ever what it was, and he asked him, said Mister, can you tell us where the monkey cage is at? Well, course it is funny now. The man he looked down at all us little colored children and we was all barefooted and as raggedy as a stump full of grandaddies and he said: If you couldnt find your way back, what did you leave for?

Ben laughs. Papaw smiles.

PAPAW We didnt know nothin about the world. Didnt know nothin. We was babes in the woods. *(He stirs his tea).* I went to work when I was twelve and it wasnt long fore I learned that a lot of what the good book said was ever bit as true as it was claimed. Stone aint so heavy as the wrath of a fool and I worked for white men and I was subjugated to that wrath many a time and I become very dissatisfied about my lot in this world. The peculiar thing was that the very thing that brought me to that pass was what led me out of it and since that time I've come to see that more often than not that's how the Lord works.

He sips his tea. They sit.

BEN What was it? That brought you to that pass and led you out of it.

PAPAW Just the work. Just the trade. That was all they was to it. All they ever was to it. I've wondered all my life what people outside of the trade do. I wonder it yet.

He sips his tea.

PAPAW I made it a study to put up with foolishness and not to be made party to it. I liked the work from the first time I ever turned to it and I was determined that they wasnt goin to run me off no matter how crazy they got and they didnt. You had black and white masons work side by side on them big jobs but you was never paid the same and you was never acknowledged the same. But I knowed Uncle Selman could lay stone to beat any man on that job didnt make no difference what color he was and anybody that didnt know it was just too ignorant to count. So I seen that he was acknowledged if he was colored and that made me think again. I seen they was some things that folks couldnt lie about. The facts was too plain. And what a man was worth at his work was one of them things. It was just knowed to everbody from the lowest to the highest and they wasnt no several opinions about it. When I seen that I seen the way my path had to go if I was ever to become the type of man I had it in my heart to be. I was twelve year old and I never looked back. Never looked back.

BEN What about when Uncle Selman was killed. Did that change your feelings?

PAPAW No. It didnt. I was older then and I seen it for what it was. A man that's killed by a fool that aint never had the first thought in his head it aint no different from if a rock fell on him. It's just a sad thing to happen and they aint no help for it.

BEN You werent set crazy over it?

PAPAW Pret near. But they wasnt no point in me goin crazy. That man was not a mason. He was in charge of settin timbers and he picked Selman out because he was a small man and Selman was a big one. It was just a dispute that they wasnt no sense to it. Cept I knowed Selman was not disputatious and you couldnt get him to argue didnt make no difference how wrong you was and I reckon that made that white man crazier than what he already was. It was a dispute over a waterbucket and that's about as sorry as you can get, I reckon. Ever crew had they own buckets and they was marked and had stripes on em for to mark the white ones from the colored's. I dont know what the particulars was but it was over them buckets and I know Uncle Selman was in the right for he never would allow no misrepresentation of nothin. You couldnt put a gun to his head and get him to lie and I dont care what kind of lie it was. He always said they was not no such a thing as a small lie. And that white man was all lie. And he killed him. He killed Uncle Selman with a timber maul, hit him blind side with it and laid him out graveyard dead. They come and got me. Oh I was a heartbroke boy. A heartbroke boy. We picked him up out of the dirt and carried him out under a shadetree and he was bloody as a hog and I just set there under that tree with him and I cried like a baby. I aint ashamed to tell it.

They sit quietly. Papaw is moved even now.

BEN What did they do with the white man?
PAPAW He left this country and he stayed gone a long time. They was fixin to law him and he just left out. The boss of that job was goin to testify against him and he told that boss man, said: You take a nigger's part against a white man's? That's what he said. And Uncle Selman laid out dead. Said: You take a nigger's part against a white man's? and that boss man—his name was Johnson—he never even answered him.
BEN But he came back?
PAPAW Yes. He come back.
BEN And what happened then?
PAPAW Nothin. He stayed gone I guess it was six or seven

year and then he come back and there was nothin ever done about it. I lawed him myself and it costed me a right smart but it was too late to bring him to justice.

They sit. Papaw stirs and rises and takes his cup and his hat and coat.

PAPAW I guess I better change out of these clothes.

He goes to the sink.

BEN What was the man's name?
PAPAW That killed Uncle Selman?
BEN Yes.
PAPAW Well. That's been a long time ago, Benny. Been a long time ago.
BEN But you remember his name.

Papaw puts his cup in the sink and turns.

PAPAW Oh yes. He has children livin in this town. Children and grandchildren. Great grandchildren.
BEN What was his name?
PAPAW Well. I guess I'd rather not to say it.

He goes to his room door and exits.

SCENE IV

The kitchen, night. The supper dishes are washed and in the drainboard. Ben is asleep at the kitchen table with his head cradled in his arms. There are steps on the basement stairs and Maven enters in her bathrobe. She goes to Ben and strokes the back of his head. He sits up and looks at her.

MAVEN Baby why dont you take your shower.

BEN He hasnt come in has he?

MAVEN No.

BEN What time is it?

MAVEN Quarter of eleven.

Ben leans back and looks up at the ceiling.

MAVEN Why dont you take your shower.

BEN I'm going to kill him.

MAVEN *(Smiling)* Come on.

Ben rises and gets his coat from the chair.

BEN I'll be back in a little bit.

MAVEN Oh Ben.

BEN I'll be back in a little bit.

SCENE V

A dimly lit door stage right. Ben knocks at the door and turns and looks out at the street. He turns and knocks at the door again. The door opens and MRS RAYMOND—*a middleaged woman in a chenille robe with her hair up in a plastic cap—opens the door and looks out.*

BEN Mrs Raymond I hate to bother you so late but I wonder if Emmett knows anything about Soldier. He hasnt been home since last night.

Mrs Raymond looks down and shakes her head.

BEN Is he still up?

MRS RAYMOND *(Turning toward inside of house)* Emmett, you see Soldier today?

EMMETT *(Offstage)* I dont know nothin bout Soldier.

MRS RAYMOND Say he dont know nothin bout him.

BEN Was he in school Friday?

MRS RAYMOND *(To Emmett)* Soldier in school Friday?

EMMETT I aint seen him.

MRS RAYMOND Say he aint seen him.

BEN What about Jeffrey. Was Jeffrey in school?

MRS RAYMOND *(To Emmett)* Jeffrey in school on Friday?

They wait. Emmett doesnt answer.

MRS RAYMOND *(To Emmett)* JEFFREY IN SCHOOL
ON FRIDAY?
EMMETT I dont know nothin bout Soldier and I dont
know nothin bout Jeffrey.
MRS RAYMOND Say he dont know nothin bout neither
one of em.

Ben looks off stage right. He looks at Mrs Raymond.

BEN Well. Thank you Mrs Raymond.
MRS RAYMOND Well.

She shuts the door.

SCENE VI

*The kitchen, morning. Mama is fixing breakfast and Carlotta is
setting the table. Big Ben is on the telephone. He is dressed in
overalls and a workshirt with long underwear showing at his collar and cuffs. There is a knocking at the door.* OSREAU *is peering
in through the glass.*

BIG BEN *(On telephone)* You tell him call Topcat or one of
them Williams boys. Well you call him then. Tell him he
dont want his job we got people standin in line.

Big Ben holds the receiver to one side and turns to the table.

BIG BEN Sister let Osreau in there. Caint you see him standin yonder? *(Into telephone)* And bring your hundred foot tape.

Carlotta goes past Big Ben to the door.

CARLOTTA You closer to the door than me.
BIG BEN *(To telephone)* All right.

He hangs up the phone. Osreau enters the kitchen. He is a black mason in his early forties, dressed in workclothes.

OSREAU Mornin. Mornin.

Big Ben crosses the kitchen on his way to the front door for the paper.

BIG BEN We havin any breakfast this mornin?
MAMA Osreau you had your breakfast?
OSREAU Yes mam.
MAMA Well set down anyway. You all come on now. Carlotta get the chair. And call Papaw. Where's Benny at?

Mama carries platters to the table. Carlotta gets the extra chair and goes to Papaw's door and calls him. Ben enters in his work-

clothes and sits down. Big Ben enters with the paper and sits at the head of the table and Papaw comes out and takes his place.

MAMA Carlotta did you want to say grace?

CARLOTTA You say it Mama.

MAMA Bless oh Lord this food to our nourishment and us to thy service. And please Lord send that boy back to his family safe and sound. We ask it in Jesus' name. Amen.

FAMILY Amen.

They raise their heads and begin to pass the platters. They eat in silence. Mama looks sideways at Carlotta who is eating woodenly. The phone rings. They freeze. They look at Carlotta. The phone rings again and she pushes back her chair and rises and goes to answer it.

CARLOTTA Hello. Hi Jenny. No. I dont know. Ben went down yesterday and filled out a report. Yes. I know you will. I'll call you. Thanks Jenny. Bye.

She hangs up the phone and turns back to the table. The rest of the family continue eating. Carlotta suddenly hurries past the table and out of the kitchen. They listen to her footsteps going up the stairs. They continue to eat. Ben wipes his mouth and gets up from the table and leaves the kitchen and goes upstairs. The lights dim in the kitchen. The lights come on stage right in Carlotta's bedroom. There is a window with white curtains and a simple bed with a ruffled white counterpane and Carlotta is sitting on the bed with her head in her hands. Ben knocks on the door.

CARLOTTA Just a minute.

She wipes her eyes and gets up and goes to the door and opens it and then turns back and begins to collect her purse and her things to go to work, keeping her eyes averted. Ben stands just inside the door watching her. Outside it is just daylight and there are early morning street sounds.

BEN We'll find him Carly. He's just pulled some dumb stunt. Chances are he'll be at school today . . .

CARLOTTA *(Turning and facing Ben)* Well if he's not in jail and not in any of the hospitals I'd like to know where you think he is.

BEN Well. I think there's a good chance he might be on his way to see Landry.

CARLOTTA Oh yeah. Fifteen year old boy on his way to Detroit in the dead of winter with maybe forty cents in his pocket.

BEN He could be.

She gives up looking through her purse and sits down on the bed and begins to cry, putting her hands to her face. Ben comes to the bed.

BEN Hey.

He sits down and puts his arms around her and she turns and puts her face on his shoulder, crying quietly.

BEN Come on Baby.

CARLOTTA Oh Ben I dont know what I'm going to do he just wont do a thing I tell him anymore and he's in trouble at school all the time and I'm so tired of this damn job and tired of living in this damn house and I want to be on my own and I cant and it's just getting worse everything's getting worse and Landry damn damn damn him he's going to get married again and I still love him and he's just a son of a bitch, Ben, and now this . . .

BEN I know Baby.

He pats her and she stops crying and sits up.

CARLOTTA I've got to go. I'm going to be late.

BEN Did he tell you he's getting married?

CARLOTTA No. He doesnt have the guts. But I know he is.

BEN Is he still sending the checks?

CARLOTTA Yes. Yes.

She gets up and collects her things. She dabs at her makeup.

BEN Why dont you go back to school?

CARLOTTA I cant afford to go to school.

BEN I told you I'd send you.

CARLOTTA I cant do that. God, you work night and day as it is.

BEN So?

CARLOTTA You've got your own family.

BEN Yes. It includes you.

CARLOTTA Besides school's not the answer to everything.

BEN No. But I know you want to go.

CARLOTTA I dont see that it's done you all that much good.

BEN Why? Because I work as a mason instead of teaching? I make three times what a teacher does.

CARLOTTA Yes, and I know how you make it too. You're killing yourself. And it's not the money anyway. —I've got to go.

She puts on her coat. He gets up from the bed.

CARLOTTA Ben if anything has happened to him I dont know what I'll do. I really dont.

BEN Nothing's happened. I promise.

CARLOTTA You cant promise. You think you can fix everything. You cant.

She goes past him to the door. In the doorway she stops and looks at herself in her compact mirror. She closes the compact and puts it in her purse. She looks at him.

CARLOTTA I look awful. Ben, thank you.

She exits.

CURTAIN

ACT III

SCENE I

The kitchen at night. It is late and the house is asleep. Ben is sitting at the table with his tea and his notebook. The light comes on at the podium. Ben speaks from there.

BEN He's not always asleep when I hear him talking in his room at night. I know his mind is sound but sometimes he forgets and I know sometimes he's half awake or even sitting on the edge of the bed talking to his brother Charles whom he loved and who fell to his death from the scaffolding at the construction of the Seelbach Hotel in the fall of 1902.

He—Ben's double—picks up Papaw's bible from the table and smells the old leather.

BEN When they were breaking ground to build the bank out on the Bardstown road there was a piece in the paper about his one hundredth birthday and his letter from President Nixon and they called him and talked to him on the phone trying to get him to lay the cornerstone at their ceremony or whatever it was and he would not and they sent the vicepresident over here to talk to him thinking there was some misunderstanding and he and Papaw sat in the front room while Mama served them coffee and Papaw was as polite as he could be and told him no about nine times and showed him to the door and Mama was furious with him and wanted to know why he wouldnt do it and he wouldnt answer and wouldnt answer and finally he said: I aint never laid a block of hewn stone in my life and I never will. You go against scripture you on you own. That man up there aint goin to help you. Aint no need to even ask.

He sips his tea and thumbs the bible open. He turns the pages.

BEN It took me a while to find that one.

He leans forward at the kitchen table, reading.

BEN And if thou make me an altar of stone thou shalt not build it of hewn stone, for if thou lift up thy tool upon it thou hast polluted it.

He turns the pages.

BEN There's another place too. Somewhere here. And all the proscribing of graven images. Why? Deuteronomy. His ribbon here. Pharoh. We were Pharoh's slaves in Egypt and the Lord brought us out of Egypt with a mighty hand.

He turns the pages.

BEN And Exodus. That there may be darkness over the land of Egypt. Egypt and the darkness of Egypt. According to the old charges of the Masonic order the children of Israel learned masonry in Egypt. Which I was astonished to read, having heard it from him, and he knows nothing of freemasonry. He says all honors are empty and none more than honorary masonry. Because there is nothing that will separate from the work itself. The work is everything, and whatever is learned is learned in the doing. The freemasons were right in their suspicion that in the mysteries of stonemasonry were contained other mysteries. Speculatives, they were called. Noblemen who were made honorary masons. And if it is true that laying stone can teach you reverence of God and tolerance of your neighbor and love for your family it is also true that this knowledge is instilled in you through the work and not through any contemplation of the work.

He rises and goes to the woodstove and adds a chunk of wood to the fire and shuts the door and stands looking at the flames through the grate.

BEN But not ashlar. Not cut stone. All trades have their origin in the domestic and their corruption in the state. Freestone masonry is the work of free men while sawing stone is the work of slaves and of course it is just those works of antiquity most admired in the history books that require nothing but time and slavery for their completion. It is a priestridden stonecraft, whether in Egypt or Peru. Or Louisville Kentucky. I'd read a great deal in the Old Testament before it occurred to me that it was among other things a handbook for revolutionaries. That what it extolls above all else is freedom. There is no historian and no archaelogist who has any conception of what stonework means. The Semitic God was a god of the common man and that is why he'll have no hewn stones to his altar. He'll have no hewing of stone because he'll have no slavery.

When I showed Papaw photographs of Mayan stonework he only shook his head. Stretchers and headers and

quoins are the very soul of stonemasonry and of these
they had none. Perhaps their mortar was mixed with
human blood as in the old ballads. Papaw knows these
tales too. He says the only blood you'll ever need is the
blood of your redeemer.

He closes the stove door and returns to the table.

BEN And the secrecy. Always the secrecy. "Whatsoever
thou hearest or seeist him do, tell it no man, wheresoever
thou go." That from Guild rules of the fourteenth cen-
tury. But it wasnt just to protect the guild. The reason the
stonemason's trade remains esoteric above all others is
that the foundation and the hearth are the soul of human
society and it is that soul that the false mason threatens.

So. It's not the mortar that holds the work together.
What holds the stone trues the wall as well and I've seen
him check his fourfoot wooden level with a plumb bob
and then break the level over the wall and call for a new
one. Not in anger, but only to safeguard the true. To
safeguard it everywhere. He says that to a man who's
never laid a stone there's nothing you can tell him. Even
the truth would be wrong. The calculations necessary to
the right placement of stone are not performed in the
mind but in the blood. Or they are like those vestibular
reckonings performed in the inner ear for standing up-

right. I see him standing there over his plumb bob which never lies and never lies and the plumb bob is pointing motionless to the unimaginable center of the earth four thousand miles beneath his feet. Pointing to a blackness unknown and unknowable both in truth and in principle where God and matter are locked in a collaboration that is silent nowhere in the universe and it is this that guides him as he places his stone one over two and two over one as did his fathers before him and his sons to follow and let the rain carve them if it can.

SCENE II

The kitchen, morning. The family has just finished breakfast and Mama is clearing away the table. Big Ben is reading the paper and Carlotta is smoking a cigarette. Ben gets up from the table. He is wearing sport clothes, not dressed for work. He goes to the sink and rinses out his cup and takes his leather jacket and puts it on. Big Ben lowers the paper and looks at him.

BIG BEN I dont know what use it be you drivin up and down the roads.

BEN I'm not going to drive up and down the roads.

Big Ben regards him over the top of his paper. Ben turns up his coat collar.

BIG BEN What did the police say?

BEN I told you what the police said.

BIG BEN You aint told me nothin.

BEN I told Mama.

BIG BEN I aint Mama.

BEN They didnt say anything. They just take down the information. They fill out a report. They dont even list them as missing until they've been gone forty-eight hours. Then they put the report in a filing cabinet along with about a thousand others, kids that are missing. Missing or misplaced or lost or people just couldnt remember where they'd left them or maybe no one even noticed they were gone or maybe they had no place to be missing from in the first place.

BIG BEN Carlotta say the truant officer callin up here wantin to know why he aint in school.

BEN Sure. You think the left hand knows what the right is doing? Five years ago they were putting us in jail for sending our kids to school, now they want to jail us for not sending them. I've got to go. I'll be over there after dinner. Tell Osreau to be carrying it up on the back side and we'll set the lintels in the morning. Mama, Bye.

Ben exits.

MAMA *(To the closed door)* Bye honey.

BIG BEN Caint tell him nothin. Drive around. Where he goin to look for the boy at? Police aint got no sense. Teachers aint got no sense. Aint nobody got any sense but him.

MAMA Well at least he tryin to do somethin.

BIG BEN What that suppose to mean?

MAMA Dont mean nothin. Mean he tryin, that's all.

BIG BEN He just showin out. What's he goin do? The boy's run off, that's all. He'll be back.

MAMA Well, you waitin on me to peck holes in Benny you better make yourself comfortable, that's all I got to say.

BIG BEN You dont need to tell me that. Nooo. You sure dont need to tell me that.

He fluffs up his paper and turns to read, quietly indignant. Carlotta stubs out her cigarette.

CARLOTTA Why are you so sure he's just run away, Daddy?

BIG BEN He's just that age. Lot of boys his age run off from home. It's just their nature. Young boy like that . . .

CARLOTTA Did you?

BIG BEN No. But I thought about it. Course back when I was comin up young boys was kept busy and out of trouble. It wasnt like now. Nooo. Sure wasnt like now. I was Soldier's age I's workin a sixty hour week just like a man.

CARLOTTA Uncle Dyson ran away.

BIG BEN He was a lot older than me. I never did even know him till I was grown.

CARLOTTA How long did he stay gone?

BIG BEN That was different.

CARLOTTA How long did he stay gone?

BIG BEN I dont know. Twenty some odd years, I reckon. But that was a whole different thing.

MAMA I dont know what you have to go and bring up Dyson for. Worry that girl more than what she is already.

BIG BEN Me? I never made the first mention of Dyson.

CARLOTTA Mama. Mama. Let it go. He's right anyway. He never made the first mention of him. I didnt even know there was such an uncle till I was in high school. Everybody in this family thinks if you dont mention something then it doesnt exist. There must be some huge skeleton left that I still dont know about. What was it? Was somebody a whore or a horsethief or vote Republican?

MAMA Now girl dont you start with that mouth.

CARLOTTA I dont know where you all get it from. Papaw's not like that.

MAMA Some things is better left unsaid. That's just common knowledge. Papaw dont tell everthing he knows.

CARLOTTA No, but he'll tell you anything you ask him.

MAMA Everbody has things they'd rather to not talk about.

CARLOTTA Well if he does I never heard it. Or maybe he'll talk about it anyway, rather or not.

MAMA Well they aint never been no criminals in this family like what you said. Not that I ever heard of. I dont know what use it be tellin everbody if they was though.

CARLOTTA Well there's a first time for everything. Right?

BIG BEN What's that supposed to mean?

Carlotta gets up from the table. She looks as if she's about to cry.

MAMA Honey it aint no crime to run off from home. You just gettin yourself all worked up now. He'll be back. You'll see. I bet Benny brings him back today.

CARLOTTA Benny this, Benny that.

She leaves the room crying. Big Ben puts down his paper and looks after her and then looks at Mama.

BIG BEN Well, that ought to satisfy you I reckon.

MAMA *(Shaking her head sadly)* No. It dont give me no satisfaction. Trouble comes to a house it comes to visit everbody. It make me cry too, Daddy. Cry for her. Cry for that boy. Cry for everbody. They sure aint no satisfaction in it.

SCENE III

Offstage sounds of running and hard breathing. The footsteps slow and then subside, the breathing continues. The lights come up on a scene stage right set with a metal slat parkbench and a streetlamp. Sounds of traffic in the distance. JEFFREY, *a young black about sixteen years of age and dressed in jeans and sneakers, is sitting on the bench gasping for breath. Ben is leaning against the lamp post, not quite so winded as Jeffrey.*

JEFFREY What you want with me man? *(He leans forward, breathing)* I aint done nothin to you.
BEN You didnt have to. I dont like you anyway.
JEFFREY *(Leaning back, turning up his eyes)* Shit.
BEN You know what I'm going to do to you?
JEFFREY Yeah.

He sits breathing.

JEFFREY What you want, man.
BEN Mr Telfair.
JEFFREY *(Looking at Ben)* Say *what?*
BEN What do you want Mr Telfair.
JEFFREY *(Leaning forward again)* Shit.
BEN Jeffrey.

JEFFREY What.

BEN I want to know what's happened to Soldier.

JEFFREY I dont know nothin bout Soldier.

BEN What did you run for?

JEFFREY What you chase me for?

BEN I want to know where he is.

JEFFREY I look like I got him?

Ben shakes his head. He looks away. He looks at Jeffrey again.

BEN Jeffrey. Jeffrey. Jeffrey this boy's mother is my sister. My only sister. If you know anything at all about where Soldier is or what's happened to him I want you to tell me. I dont care how bad it is.

JEFFREY I dont know where he is and that's the truth.

BEN What happened to the Newman boy.

JEFFREY *(Looking down, shaking his head)* Aw man. I got to listen to this again?

BEN What happened to him.

JEFFREY I dont know what happened to the boy. He died.

BEN He died.

JEFFREY The boy got his ticket punched. That's all I know. What would I know about it? Shit man. He's a fourteen year old kid. I didnt even know who he was till this shit started.

BEN What happened to the Nighthawks?

JEFFREY Nighthawks? Aint no Nighthawks no more.

BEN Your brother used to be president.

JEFFREY So what's that make me?

BEN You tell me.

JEFFREY *(Leaning back and looking at Ben)* You dont know shit man. They aint no more Nighthawks. Aint no more clubs. They aint shit. Just a bunch of freelancers out roguin and doin drugs. These young bloods are all strung out, man. You understand what I'm tellin you? Fourteen year old. Twelve. You leanin all over me bout some young dude got killed. Shit. It's just brother against brother. Shit goin down out there dont make no more sense than nothin. Try and tell these young bloods bout the Nighthawks. They look at you like you from Mars, man.

BEN *(Watching Jeffrey)* How old are you, Jeffrey?

JEFFREY Sixteen.

BEN How old do you think I am?

JEFFREY Man I dont know how old you are. All I know is you livin in the past. I'm livin in the past. History done swallowed you up cept you dont know it.

BEN If history swallows everybody up who do you think is running the world?

JEFFREY It look to you like somebody *runnin* it?

BEN When I was sixteen I looked forward to being eighteen. I looked forward to being twenty-one.

JEFFREY Yeah, well. Everbody over sixteen the same age to me. And I feel like I'm a hundred.

SCENE IV

Night. The kitchen. Ben sits at the table drinking tea. Lights sweep across the window from outside and a car pulls in and stops and a door opens and slams. Big Ben enters the kitchen. He takes off his hat and his camelhair overcoat. He is dressed in a suit with a sportshirt open at the neck.

BEN Hey.

Big Ben crosses heavily to the stove.

BIG BEN They any coffee?
BEN I think there is. You'll have to warm it.

Big Ben shakes the pot and sets it on the burner and turns on the stove.

BIG BEN Well. We got trouble.
BEN We do?
BIG BEN It's your company too.
BEN Well what's the trouble.

BIG BEN I need six thousand dollars is what the trouble is.

BEN Oh man.

Ben looks down. He shakes his head slowly. He looks up at Big Ben again.

BEN Six *thousand?*

Big Ben looks at Ben. He swirls the coffee pot and sets it back down again.

BEN Cant you get it from the bank?

BIG BEN They say I caint.

BEN You've borrowed money from them before.

BIG BEN They wont let me have no more.

BEN What do you mean no more?

BIG BEN Mean no more. Say they aint goin let me have no more.

He gets a cup down from the shelf. He swirls the pot and pours coffee into the cup.

BEN How much do you owe them?

BIG BEN Dont make no difference bout that. The facts is that I got to have six thousand dollars come next Wednesday.

BEN What happens if you dont? What are they going to foreclose on?

BIG BEN Aint a matter of foreclosure.

BEN Well why dont you explain it to me a step at a time.

BIG BEN Only thing needs explainin is I got to have the money.

BEN Why dont you tell me what it is you've done.

BIG BEN *(Angrily)* I aint done a damn thing. I just need the money.

BEN Well where do you think I'm going to get six thousand dollars?

BIG BEN You can get it. They'd let you have it.

BEN You're talking about me mortgaging the farm.

Big Ben doesnt answer. He stands leaning against the stove.

BEN It's not mine to mortgage.

BIG BEN Whose is it if it aint yours?

BEN It's in a trust.

BIG BEN You aint goin to help me.

BEN I'm not going to mortgage that property. I couldnt if I wanted to. Cant you borrow against the house?

BIG BEN No.

BEN Why not?

BIG BEN I done borrowed against it.

There is a silence in the room.

BEN Are you going to lose the house?

BIG BEN No.

BEN You are, arent you?

BIG BEN *(Angrily)* I dont get some money I'm goin to lose everthing I got.

Silence.

BEN *(Quietly)* I'll go to the bank tomorrow. I'll see what they'll let me have on an unsecured note. They'll want Maven to cosign though. And I dont think they're going to let me have any six thousand dollars. How much does Mama know about this?

BIG BEN She dont need to know nothin.

BEN Well, when they put her in the street she'll know. Her and her shoes. I always wondered why she had about forty pair of shoes. She's a provident woman.

BIG BEN Well pile it all on my head. You and Pap both just walked off and left the company. Just walked off and left it.

BEN I give you forty hours a week. Every week. Papaw worked on the job every day till he was ninety-two years old. What do you want?

Big Ben drains his cup and puts it in the sink and crosses to the chair and gets his hat and coat.

BIG BEN Dont make no difference what I want. I aint goin to get it. Not even in my own house. Under my own roof. Never could and never will.

He exits the kitchen. His steps on the stairs.

SCENE V

The kitchen, morning. Ben and Maven are sitting at the table. Maven is dressed for school. Mama is putting away cups and dishes out of the drainboard. She finishes and comes to the table and picks up the morning paper.

MAMA You done with this Benny?
BEN Yes mam.

She takes the paper and shuffles on toward the door.

MAMA Take my bath.
BEN Mama, do you read the paper in the bathtub?
MAMA You dont need to be speculatin bout what I does in the bathtub.

She goes out the door and up the stairs. Ben smiles. He looks at Maven. She smiles.

BEN Arent you going to be late?
MAVEN No. Yes. Probably.

She looks at her cup and she looks up at Ben. Ben raises his chin in a gesture that means Let's hear it.

MAVEN I dont know. The basement's not far enough away any more.
BEN I know.
MAVEN I dont know what to say to Carlotta any more. I really dont.

Ben purses his lips and nods.

MAVEN Ben, how much money does your father owe you?

He looks up at Maven.

BEN I dont know. I'd have to look it up.
MAVEN But you know more or less.
BEN Yes. I just dont want you to worry about it.
MAVEN I worry anyway.
BEN Do you want me to tell you?

MAVEN Yes.

BEN It's around eleven thousand dollars.

Maven sits looking at her cup.

BEN Well?

She shakes her head. She looks up at Ben.

MAVEN Has business been that bad?

BEN No.

MAVEN Does he underbid the jobs?

BEN All black contractors underbid the jobs. If they didnt they wouldnt get the work. But that's not it.

MAVEN Well what does he do with the money?

BEN I dont know.

MAVEN If you got paid for the work you do you could hire somebody out at the farm. You mix your own mud out there.

BEN I have no argument against you.

MAVEN Well I dont think you should let him take advantage of you just because he's your father.

BEN I know. Every Friday is a shoot-out. You dont know. If you think you hear a lot of poormouthing around here you ought to hear him on the job.

Maven gets up and takes her cup and saucer to the sink. She comes back to the table and kisses Ben on the forehead and takes her coat off the chair.

BEN Is that it?

MAVEN *(Taking up her briefcase from the chair)* That's it, Babe.

Ben shakes his head, smiling. She starts for the door and then turns.

MAVEN Ben.

He juts his chin at her to say yes.

MAVEN What do you think has happened to Soldier?

BEN I dont know.

MAVEN If it was something terrible and you didnt want me to know and I wanted to know would you tell me?

BEN Yes.

MAVEN I want to know.

BEN I dont know what's happened to him. I just dont know. He may come back. He may be dead. I just dont know.

MAVEN Would you tell Carlotta? If it was something terrible and there was nothing anyone could do about it?

BEN I dont know. I dont think so. Maybe I'd be wrong. I dont think I could.

She bends and kisses him.

MAVEN Bye.
BEN Bye, Lady.

CURTAIN

ACT IV

―――――――――

SCENE I

Night, the kitchen. Ben at the table drinking tea. The light comes on at the podium and Ben takes his place there.

BEN He didnt come back. Mama walked around the house like a Roman stoic for weeks just as if she'd not a worry in the world and then one night she woke from a dream or from I dont know what and she cried straight through till breakfast and she would not be consoled and we brought her down to the kitchen and Maven wanted to call the doctor and my father tried to give her whiskey and all she would say was that poor child, that poor child. And Maven was right. It's worse than a death. More vengeful than a suicide. His absence is like a pall of guilt and humiliation. People would say He'll come back. Or He'll turn up. Then they stopped saying anything. Then they stopped coming around. Carlotta for a long time would not come to the dinnertable and we ate in silence and then she did come and we ate in more silence. His birthday is in two more weeks. He would be sixteen. Will be sixteen? In what tense do you speak of those who have vanished? You dont speak of them. You are simply enslaved to them. And Carlotta was right. I think I can fix everything. The simplest word of consolation sounds like a lie. She was right about Landry too. He did get married.

INTERMISSION

SCENE II

The light is on in the front room and in the kitchen. It is evening and Ben comes in the kitchen door and puts the kettle on and goes through and into the front room to get the paper. A young man is sitting rather formally in the front room waiting for Carlotta. He is dressed in a suit and tie. Ben goes through and gets the paper and shuts the outer door offstage and returns with the paper. The visitor stands up. His name is MASON FERGUSON.

MASON Hello. I'm Mason Ferguson.

He holds out his hand and he and Ben shake hands.

MASON I met you once before.

BEN Mason, what are you doing sitting in here all by yourself?

MASON I'm waiting for Carlotta.

BEN Well you better come on in the kitchen.

Mason follows him into the kitchen. Ben throws the paper on the table and goes to the stove.

BEN Sit down. What can I get you?

MASON Not a thing, thank you.

BEN I can give you coffee or tea or a beer. Or a Coke.

MASON No thanks. Really.

BEN *(Getting down teabags)* Well I'm just getting ready to have a cup of tea. Do you drink tea?

MASON Well, yes.

BEN Good.

He gets down cups.

BEN What sort of work do you do, Mason?

MASON I'm an insurance claims adjuster.

BEN *(Pouring water in the cups)* Claims adjuster. You want lemon?

MASON No thank you.

Ben brings the cups to the table and takes a chair opposite Mason.
He sips his tea.

BEN There's sugar there.

MASON This is fine.

BEN Well, you look sober and industrious. Have you ever
been married?

MASON No.

BEN *(Smiling)* You can stop me any time you want.

MASON *(Smiling)* That's okay.

BEN Does she like you?

MASON I beg your pardon?

BEN Does she like you? Carly. Does she like you.

MASON *(Laughing a little nervously)* Well. I dont know.
Maybe you should ask her.

BEN But you hope she likes you.

MASON Yes.

Ben smiles and sips his tea. Mason smiles.

MASON You didnt ask me if I like her.

BEN I know you like her. I knew you liked her when I saw
you in there sitting on the sofa.

Mason smiles. Footsteps on the stairs overhead.

BEN Here she comes. I'll ask her.

MASON Ask her what?

BEN If she likes you.

MASON Hey, come on.

BEN You said I should ask her.

MASON *(Smiling)* Hey, dont fool around.

Carlotta comes in the kitchen. Ben laughs. Mason pushes back his chair and rises.

MASON Hi.

CARLOTTA *(Looking at Ben)* Ben, you leave him alone.

BEN Hey Babe. Mmm, you look good.

He turns to Mason.

CARLOTTA Ben.

BEN *(Laughing)* Hey, we were getting along like a house afire. Werent we, Mason.

MASON Yes. We were.

BEN I think this is one of the better ones you've had in here all week.

CARLOTTA You know, I dont think I could bring myself to actually shoot you. But poison's not out of the question.

Ben regards her more seriously.

BEN You're such a pretty lady.

Carlotta is a little flustered. She turns to Mason.

CARLOTTA Are you ready?
MASON Mmm-hmm. Ben, good to see you.

Ben rises and they shake hands.

BEN You all have a good time.

Ben watches them exit out the kitchen door.

SCENE III

The kitchen at night. Ben at the kitchen table with his cup of tea and his notebook. The light comes on at the podium and Ben takes his place there.

BEN That summer Papaw and I contracted work on our own, just working evenings and weekends. We still worked on the house at the farm too but we were building old style stone chimneys and fireplaces for people and we'd take them on field trips and show them the old work and if they had souls in their bodies they would see all that we showed them and we were amazed at how quickly a love and a reverence for reality could be restored in them. They'd talk about what they wanted and Papaw would say little and smoke his pipe and they would look at some old chimney standing in a field and they would look at Papaw and they would grow more quiet themselves and then they would stop talking altogether and we would drive back and they'd ask us when we could begin. Sometimes if a client was really interested we'd take him all over the county. We'd show him work that Papaw had done eighty years ago. We'd show them walls and cellars and chimneys and houses and springhouses and bridges. Some of those old cellars and footings contain enormous stones and Papaw says it's because the houses were built first and you had scaffolding and teams of oxen and tackle and men and you could use the big stones but when you were building a wall you were pretty much on your own and you did it as you could. Most of the old slave walls as they are called were built in the winter when farm work was light. But I've seen stones in cellars and in the base of chimneys that would weigh two thousand pounds. I've seen old bridge piers built of rubble stone weighing two and three tons apiece and no two stones alike and laid up without mortar sixteen and eighteen courses high and steeply battered. I've looked at barns and houses and bridges and factories and chimneys and walls and in a thousand structures I've never seen a misplaced stone. In form and design and scale and structure and proportion I've yet to see an example of the old work that was not perfectly executed. They were designed by the men who built them and their design rose out of necessity. The beauty of those structures would appear to be just a sort of a by-product, something fortuitous, but of course it is not. The aim of the mason was to make the wall stand up and that was his purpose in its entirety. The beauty of the stonework is simply a reflection of the purity of the mason's intention. Carly says I have this mystique thing about stonemasonry. She says nobody understands it. Even my father thinks it's crazy. She says no one knows what I'm talking about. She says no one cares. In all this of course she's right. And she says you cant change history and that ruins should be left to ruin. And she's right. But that the craft of stonemasonry should be allowed to vanish from this world is just not negotiable for me. Somewhere there is someone who wants to know. Nor will I have to seek him out. He'll find me.

SCENE IV

The kitchen, afternoon. GUESTS *and their* CHILDREN *in Sunday clothes are leaving, going out through the living room. Mama is saying goodbye to cousins and other kin and a* PHOTOGRAPHER *thanks her and shoulders up his camera and tripod and exits. Maven is nine months pregnant. Ben is in the kitchen talking to a* REPORTER. *The other guests all leave and the lights dim out in the living room and Mama goes upstairs and Maven goes to the basement apartment.*

REPORTER *(Looking through his small notepad)* His name is spelled conventionally isnt it?

BEN Yes. Just Edward. There wasnt any creative spelling back them. Blacks couldnt spell.

REPORTER I guess that's right.

BEN He was a grown man before he learned to read and write. His wife taught him. My grandmother.

REPORTER Where did she learn?

BEN She taught herself.

REPORTER I would think that would be hard to do.

BEN I would too. She worked for a family as a live-in maid in Evansville Indiana and they had twin daughters about school age and after she got them put to bed at night she'd sit down with their primers [prim-ers] and study by candlelight until one and two in the morning and then get up again at five-thirty and get breakfast for the family. She did that for several years and then one day the woman—the lady of the house—went in her room and found some of their books there. My grandmother had a room up over the carriage house and she'd sneak books out of the house and read them at night and this woman found them and thought she was stealing the books to sell them—back then books were valuable—and she was going to fire her and my grandmother sat down and read for her and she let her stay.

REPORTER She must have been a remarkable woman.

BEN She was. Later she was the first black registered nurse in the state of Indiana. But she read all her life. And she remembered what she read. She could quote poetry by the hour. She could quote Scott's *Lady of the Lake* in its entirety and it runs about a hundred pages. When I was in high school she used to help me with my algebra. It never occurred to me to wonder where she learned it.

REPORTER And your grandfather. Does he read?

BEN (*Smiling*) Constantly.

REPORTER What does he read.

BEN The King James version of the bible.

REPORTER Is that it?

BEN That's it.

REPORTER You said he read constantly.

BEN He does.

The reporter nods and smiles.

REPORTER Well. He certainly seems to be in remarkable health for a man a hundred and two years old. I know he gets tired of people asking him the secret of his longevity but I couldnt get anything out of him at all. He just said that somebody had to live to be a hundred and it looked like it was him. My guess is that it runs in the family.

BEN Well. Not really. He had several brothers and sisters and they've all been dead for years. For that matter all his children are dead except my father.

REPORTER I asked him how his health was and he said it was fine and wanted to know how mine was. I thought at first he was being cantankerous but he really seemed to want to know. I wound up telling him about my eye operation.

Ben smiles. The reporter flips through his notebook and folds it away in his coat pocket. He holds out his hand.

REPORTER Well, thank you. It was a great party.

BEN *(Shaking hands)* Thank you for coming.

The reporter has turned to leave and then looks back.

REPORTER What is the trade? He mentioned a couple of times something about the trade.

BEN The stonemason's trade.

REPORTER Ah. Of course. Got it.

The reporter raises a hand and exits from the kitchen. Ben goes to the window and looks out. The lights come on stage right where there are picnic tables covered with red crepe and there are lanterns and foldingchairs and cups and plates and the remainders of Papaw's birthday party. A wind has come up and it is evening and the buntings strung across the yard sway in the wind and a few cups blow across the yard. Papaw is sitting alone at the tables, dressed in his black suit. His hat sits on the table beside him and he holds it with one hand against it being blown away. The lights have dimmed to black in the kitchen. The light comes on at the podium and Ben appears there.

BEN I'd pretend ignorance to get you to stay. If I thought you could be fooled. But only people with wants can be fooled and you have none.

Cups and leaves blow across the yard. The old man sits holding his hat. The light dims to black and the light comes up in the kitchen. It is night and Ben's double is sitting at the table. Ben continues to speak from the podium.

BEN He always said the trade. As if there were only the one. He didnt even call it masonry. Just called it the work. Called it the trade. Does call it. Does call it.

He—Ben's double—sips his tea.

BEN He was a journeyman mason for eighty-odd years. Journeyman comes from the word for day, and a journey was originally a day's travel. He began to contract for himself before my father married and he and my father were in business together for thirty years and technically they are yet. But the rule of the journeyman is his rule even now and he has always quit at quitting time no matter where he was on the job. The wisdom of the journeyman is to work one day at a time and he always said that any job even if it took years was made up out of a day's work. Nothing more. Nothing less. That was hard for me to learn. I always wanted to be finished. In the concept of a day's work is rhythm and pace and wholeness. And truth and justice and peace of mind. You're smiling. I smile. But very often now the stones come to hand for me as they do for him. I dont think or select. I build. So I begin to live in the world. Nothing is ever finally arrived at. The journeyman becomes a master when he masters the journeyman's trade. He becomes a master when he ceases to wish to be one.

Ben folds shut his notebook and folds his hands in front of his cup.

BEN As for the rest. As for the rest. I know that evil exists. I think it is not selective but only opportunistic. I dont know where the spirit resides. I think in all things rather than none. My experience is very limited. But it is because of him that I am no longer reduced by these mysteries but rather am one more among them. His life is round and whole but it is not discrete. Because it is connected to a way of life which he exemplifies but which is not his invention. I know nothing of God. But I know that something knows. Something knows or else that old man could not know. Something knows and will tell you. It will tell you when you stop pretending that you know.

MAVEN *(Calling from downstairs)* Ben! Ben!

Ben looks up and smiles.

SCENE V

The scene at stage left is the interior of a church, at a baptismal font, the black MINISTER *holding the baby and giving the blessing. The minister hands the baby to Papaw and Papaw and Ben (his double) and Maven and Mama turn to have their picture taken. Carlotta and Mason are in the front pew with Big Ben and Osreau and other* RELATIVES. *They come forward now that the ceremony is over. A black* WORKER *in overalls comes forward from the rear of the crowd and looks at the baby.*

WORKER What's his name, Ben?
MAMA Edward. His name is Edward.

SCENE VI

The kitchen at night. Papaw is sitting at the table, his bible and his teacup at his elbow. He is leaning forward with his head cradled in his arms apparently asleep. Ben enters the kitchen and smiles to see him and goes to the sink and fills the kettle and puts it on the stove.

BEN Papaw?

He turns the heat on under the kettle and comes to the table and puts his hand on the old man's arm.

BEN Papaw.

He puts his hand over the old man's hand.

BEN Papaw?

He sits down, holding the old man's hand. Tears run down his cheeks.

BEN *(Almost whispering)* Oh Papaw. I didnt want you to go. *(Shaking his head)* I didnt want you to go.

SCENE VII

Papaw's bedroom, stage right. A small iron bed with a nightstand and a lamp. Papaw is lying on the bed and Ben is sitting in a chair alongside the bed. Ben is asleep with his head resting on the bed in the crook of his arm. He is holding Papaw's hand. The lights come up and it is morning and he wakes. There are steps on the stairs and Mama enters the kitchen humming a spiritual and turns on the kitchen lights and begins to prepare breakfast. Ben puts his left hand on the old man's hand and withdraws his right hand from the old man's grasp and stands and looks down at him and bends and kisses him on the forehead and turns and goes into the kitchen as Mama finishes humming the piece. Mama turns and sees him standing there.

BEN Mama.

She shakes her head no. Her mouth is trembling.

BEN Mama.
MAMA Oh no. Benny. Benny. Oh no. Not that man. No.
BEN Mama.
MAMA *(Shaking her head no)* No. No.

Ben crosses the floor and puts his arms around her and she begins to wail openly.

MAMA Oh Lord Jesus no dont take that sweet man. Dont take him. Dont take him.
BEN Mama. Mama. He's already gone, Mama.

SCENE VIII

The church interior again, stage left. The family stands in front of the pew and the minister stands before them reading from the bible. The ladies wear veiled hats.

MINISTER And he called his son Joseph and said unto him If now I have found grace in thy sight put I pray thee thy hand under my thigh and deal kindly and truly with me. Bury me not I pray thee in Egypt. But I will lie with my fathers and thou shall carry me out of Egypt and bury me in their burying place. And he said I will do as thou hast said.

SCENE IX

The kitchen, mid day. Mama is on the telephone. A car pulls in the driveway. Mama looks out the window. The car door opens and closes.

MAMA Well. I got to go, Louise. Here come Ben in the middle of the day. I expect he be wantin somethin to eat. Well.

She hangs up the phone and Big Ben enters the kitchen. He is dressed in a lightcolored suit with a shirt and tie. He looks at her without expression.

MAMA Honey did you want somethin to eat?

He crosses the room and exits and goes up the stairs.

MAMA I'm goin to fix you some of that pepper steak.

The light comes on stage right which is Big Ben and Mama's bedroom. There is a double bed and a night table and a door which leads to the bathroom offstage. Big Ben enters and sits on the bed. He takes an envelope out of his pocket and tears it in several pieces and puts the pieces on the table. He opens the table drawer and takes out a revolver and puts it on the table. He rises and goes into the bathroom and turns on the light. It is a very white light that comes from the bathroom and there is the sound of water running and then he comes back into the room and begins to undress. He puts his watch and billfold on the table. He hangs his suit carefully on a hanger together with his tie and lays it across the bed. He crumples his shirt and throws it in the corner and he takes off his shoes and takes off his socks and garters and puts them in the shoes and puts the shoes under the bed. Then he rises, dressed only in very clean white shorts and undershirt and takes up the revolver and goes into the bathroom and shuts the door. Mama has been busy at the stove. She is reaching up to the shelf for the pepper when the sound of the shot reaches her. She freezes, then lowers her hand and turns to look at the door stage left. She crosses the kitchen.

MAMA Ben? Ben?

She crosses to the door.

MAMA Ben? That was outside wasnt it? That was outside wasnt it honey?

She exits and goes up the stairs.

CURTAIN

ACT V

———— ██████ ————

SCENE I

The kitchen. It is empty. The woodstove remains although the stove pipe is lying in the floor. The windows have been boarded over. Ben's pickup pulls into the drive and the truck door opens and closes and the kitchen door opens and Ben enters. He leaves the door open. He stands in the kitchen and looks around, then goes out and up the stairs. The light comes on stage right where the naked iron bedstead is the only piece of furniture left in Big Ben's bedroom. Ben comes through the room and comes around the bed and sits slowly on the bedsprings and looks out, his hands clasped, his elbows on his knees. The light comes on at the podium.

BEN The big elm tree died. The old dog died. Things that you can touch go away forever. I dont know what that means. I dont know what it means that things exist and then exist no more. Trees. Dogs. People. *Will* that namelessness into which we vanish then taste of us? The world was before man was and it will be again when he is gone. But it was not this world nor will it be, for where man lives is in this world only.

Ultimately there is no one to tell you if you are justified in your own house.

The people I know who are honorable never think about it. I think of little else.

If I'd ransomed everything and given it all to him would it have saved him?

No.

Was I obligated to do so?

Yes.

Why did you not?

Ben sitting on the bed, lowers his head.

BEN Papaw. Papaw.

Why were you everything to me and nothing to him?

SCENE II

Stage left. Ben is standing on the porch of a small frame house. It is night and the porch light is on. He taps at the door (again). The door opens and MARY WEAVER—*a woman in her midforties, not unattractive, looks out at him. She is wearing a housedress but she is well groomed.*

BEN Hello. Are you Mary Weaver?

She studies him. She nods her head.

MARY I guess you're Benny.
BEN Yes mam.
MARY I caint do nothin for you child. Let the dead sleep.
BEN I just wondered if I could talk to you for a minute.
MARY What would be the use in it?

Ben looks away. He gestures futiley. He is almost crying.

BEN I'm not here to bother you Mrs Weaver.

She shakes her head resignedly. She looks up at him. She pushes open the door.

MARY Come on in.

He enters and she closes the door and goes past him to a kitchen table with two chairs.

MARY You want a glass of iced tea?
BEN Yes mam. That would be fine.

She goes past him just offstage. She returns with a pitcher and two glasses.

MARY And quit callin me mam. I aint that old. This is done got sugar in it.
BEN That's all right.
MARY Well set down.

She pours the glasses. He sits. She takes her cigarettes from her housedress pocket and puts them on the table and sits down.

BEN Thank you.

He sips the tea. She watches him. She sighs and reaches for the cigarettes.

MARY What did you want me to tell you?

BEN Anything that you'd be willing to. About my father. Anything . . .

MARY You talk like he died fore you was born.

She lights a cigarette and studies him through the smoke.

MARY I knew when I seen you standin there you didnt know what it was you wanted.

BEN I guess I dont. It's just that you're about the only person he knew that I didnt and I kept thinking that there must be somebody . . . there must be somebody . . .

MARY I dont know why that poor man killed hisself.

BEN No. I guess you dont.

MARY Do you?

BEN *(Shaking his head)* No.

They sit. She smokes.

BEN I dont know anything about him. You live with someone all your life. All their life . . . My sister's boy. Fifteen years old. I thought he was just a troublesome kid. He was involved in things I hardly knew existed. The things I found out I couldnt believe. Yet they were so. They were so.

MARY Do you want to know what kind of man your father

was? I knew him for ten years. Did you want to know that he was kind and sweet and generous? And a real man too. Because he was. Or did you come here to find out about yourself.

He looks at her. He smiles. His eyes are wet.

BEN I dont know. Maybe.

MARY What did he say about me. What did he say about me.

BEN No.

MARY He never liked to talk about things once they was over and done with. I see you dont favor him in that respect leastways.

She carefully stubs out the cigarette.

MARY It wasnt the money. Been the money he been dead years ago. He always had money troubles. Died owin me four hundred dollar.

BEN I'll see that you get it.

MARY What for? You dont owe it. I dont want it noway.

BEN He never talked about his family?

MARY Very seldom. Very seldom. Only thing I ever remember him to say that told me a little about his deeper thought was that he'd had two brothers and a sister and they was all dead. Him bein the baby of the family I think he felt alone in the world someway. He was not a happy man, Benny. Never was. If he had of been I wouldnt of had him.

BEN Did his father dying have anything to do with it?

MARY I believe it did. But not the way you might think.

Ben looks at her. She lights another cigarette.

MARY I think maybe when his daddy died that give him leave to go on and do what he done.

BEN You dont think he could of done it with his father alive.

She blows out smoke and shakes her head.

MARY No. No way.

BEN But not his wife and children.

MARY Not his wife and children. Maybe it ought to be the same thing, but it aint. You ought to know about that. That's why you here aint it? Cause you caint get around that daddy? Caint get around that daddy.

SCENE III

BEN Because I thought of my father in death more than I ever did in life. And think of him yet. The weight of the dead makes a great burden in this world. And I know all of him that I will ever know. Why could he not see the worth of that which he had put aside and the poverty of all he hungered for? Why could he not see that he too was blest?

At times I think I came to the life of the laborer as the anchorite to his cell and pallet. The work devours the man and devours his life and I thought that in the end he must be somehow justified thereby. That if enough of the world's weight only pass through his hands he must become inaugurated into the reality of that world in a way to withstand all scrutiny. A way not easily dissolved or set aside. Perhaps in his final avatar he might even come to sit holding his hat at a wooden foldingtable borrowed from a church basement watching the wind cross the world, already beyond wind or world or anything which they might propagate or anything at all.

I lost my way. I'd thought by my labors to stand outside that true bend of gravity which is the world's pain. I lost my way and if I could tell you the hour of it or the day or how it came about I should not have lost it at all. Soldier did come back. He came back and we met secretly and I gave him money and sent him away again. Yet even before any of this I had a dream and this dream was a cautionary dream and a dream I did not heed.

In my dream I had died or the world had ended and I stood waiting before the door of some ultimate justice which I knew would open for me. I stood with my job-book beneath my arm in which were logged the hours and the days and the years and wherein was ledgered down each sack of mortar and each perch of stone and I stood alone in that whitened forecourt beyond which waited the God of all being and I stood in the full folly of my own righteousness and I took the book from under my arm and I thumbed it through a final time as if to reassure myself and when I did I saw that the pages were yellowed and crumbling and the ink faded and the accounts no longer clear and suddenly I thought to myself fool fool do you not see what will be asked of you? How He will lean down perhaps the better to see you, regarding perhaps with something akin to wonder that which is his own handiwork, He whom the firmament itself has not power to puzzle. Gazing into your soul beyond bone or flesh to its uttermost nativity in stone and star and in the unformed magma at the core of creation. And ask as you stand there alone with your book—perhaps not even unkindly—this single question: Where are the others? Where are the others. Oh I've had time in great abundance to reflect upon that terrible question. Because we cannot save ourselves unless we save all ourselves. I had this dream but did not heed it. And so I lost my way.

The diningroom at the farmhouse. There is a long diningroom table and chairs, an antique sideboard. The table is partly cleared and Mama enters and takes up more plates and carries them out to the kitchen. Ben is sitting at the head of the table and Maven and Mason are sitting at the table and Carlotta enters and takes up some dishes to carry them to the kitchen. She is about seven months pregnant. The telephone rings and Maven starts to get up but Ben motions to her to sit down.

BEN I'll get it, Babe.

He comes to the telephone and picks it up and says hello and then listens.

BEN *(To telephone)* No. No. You stay where you are. I'll be down there in twenty minutes.

He pauses and listens.

BEN Listen to me. Stay where you are. I'll be there in twenty minutes.

He hangs up the phone and returns to the table. He bends and kisses Maven.

MAVEN What is it, Ben?

BEN Got to go, Babe. I'll be back in a couple of hours.

MAVEN Oh Ben . . .

BEN *(Holding up his hand to Mason, his other hand on Maven's shoulder)* Mason.

MAVEN *(Turning)* What is it?

BEN Just something that's come up. Somebody in trouble. It's nothing really. But I have to go.

MAVEN Are they in jail?

BEN Not yet. *(He smiles)* I'll call you if I need your services.

He exits.

SCENE IV

A cheap hotel room in the central city at stage right. A nineteen year old black youth is lying on an old fashioned bed with an iron bedstead. He is dressed in cheap flashy clothes. He has a thin moustache and he is smoking a cigarette. Street sounds from below. There is a knock at the door and he gets up and goes to the door and opens it. Ben is standing at the door.

BEN Hello Soldier.

SOLDIER What say, Ben. Long time no see. Come in.
  Come in.

*Ben enters and looks around. Soldier shuts the door and motions
him to a straightback chair sitting opposite the bed. Soldier sits on
the bed and stubs out the cigarette in an ashtray on the night
table.*

SOLDIER Set down, Ben, set down.

Ben sits in the chair.

SOLDIER I went by the house. I seen they was other people
  livin there.

He looks up at Ben.

SOLDIER Dont worry. I wasnt comin in. You out at the
  farm now.

BEN We've been out there about two years.

SOLDIER Yeah, well.

Ben studies Soldier.

BEN You've been in jail.

SOLDIER Shit. Put me in no jail.

BEN It's been about a year. I knew what had happened when the checks started coming back.

SOLDIER Well, I see you aint changed. Still know everthing.

BEN Everything you've got on is new.

SOLDIER Shit.

BEN I guess that's why you're here.

SOLDIER Why's that?

BEN To collect your checks.

SOLDIER Afraid I need a little more than them checks.

Ben looks at him.

SOLDIER I'm gettin married.

BEN Getting married.

SOLDIER Yeah.

Ben shakes his head. He looks around the room. He looks at Soldier.

BEN Does she know you kill people?

SOLDIER I aint never killed nobody.

BEN You were involved in it.

SOLDIER That was a long time ago. You dont know.

BEN How much does she know about you?

Soldier laughs and shakes his head.

SOLDIER You somethin, aint you? What, you think you goin to blackmail me back? She knows all about me, sucker. She knows shit they dont nobody know.

BEN What's her name?

SOLDIER You dont need to know her name.

BEN How old is she?

SOLDIER Old enough.

BEN Where's she from?

SOLDIER She aint from here.

Ben studies Soldier.

BEN How much money do you want?

SOLDIER I need about three thousand dollars to see me right.

BEN All right.

SOLDIER Should of asked for more.

BEN I knew about what it was going to cost me.

SOLDIER Yeah. I keep forgettin bout all this shit you know.

BEN I'll bring you the money in the morning. As soon as the banks open.

He rises.

SOLDIER You dont have a little advance on that, do you?

Ben reaches in his sidepocket and takes out a money clip and peels off some bills and lays them on the night table.

BEN I'll see you here at ten in the morning.

He opens the door. Soldier rises.

SOLDIER What's this dude like that Mama married?
BEN You wouldnt like him.
SOLDIER Yeah?
BEN *(Shaking his head)* You wouldnt like him.

He pulls the door shut after him.

SCENE V

The farmhouse diningroom at night. Ben and Maven are sitting at the table.

MAVEN I wish you hadnt told me.
BEN I know.
MAVEN Why did you?
BEN I dont know. You told me you wanted to know.
MAVEN I did?
BEN A long time ago.

MAVEN I dont remember.

BEN I do.

MAVEN But you did hide it from me.

BEN I was wrong.

MAVEN Why did you wait till now?

BEN I knew what you'd say.

MAVEN Do you think you have to tell me everything?

BEN Yes.

MAVEN Why?

BEN Because. Because the smallest crumb can devour us.

MAVEN Is the world really such a hostile place?

BEN I dont know. I know that I see failure on every side and I'm determined not to fail.

MAVEN Do you think it's fair to Carlotta? You cant think that.

BEN I dont. I think it's merciful.

MAVEN Why is it up to you?

BEN Isnt it up to him?

MAVEN You have an answer for everything.

Ben doesnt answer.

MAVEN Is he really so bad?

BEN I dont know. Yes. He is. I try to give him the benefit of the doubt but there isnt any doubt.

MAVEN Maybe he'll change.

BEN I dont rule that out. I just think he should do it somewhere else.

MAVEN Somewhere else is where he got the way he is now.

BEN *(Shaking his head)* No he didnt. He got that way right here. In this family. Nowhere else.

They sit.

MAVEN If that were true wouldnt it be all the more reason . . .

BEN All the more.

MAVEN But you wont change your mind, will you?

BEN I dont feel wrong. I just feel guilty.

They sit.

MAVEN What about Mama, Ben?

BEN What indeed.

SCENE VI

The hotel room. Soldier is lying on the bed in his underclothes. He has his mouth open and he is dead. A syringe and a length of small rubber tubing lie on the night table. A burned-out book of matches. A spoon. Street sounds. The cooing of a pigeon. There is repeated knocking at the door. Finally the door opens and Ben enters. He comes in very slowly and surveys the scene. He comes to the bed and puts a hand to Soldier's neck. He picks up the spoon, the syringe. He lets them fall again. His mouth is compressed in anger and in sorrow. He pulls the chair up to the bed and sits down and holds his face in his hands. The pigeon calls. After a while Ben gets up. He looks down at Soldier. He takes the paraphernalia from the night table and puts the items in the sidepocket of his jacket. He looks around the room. Then he takes Soldier's trousers from off the footrail of the bed and goes through them and takes out his billfold and puts that in his jacket pocket. He stands looking down at Soldier. Then he turns off the bedside lamp. There is just the light from the window. The pigeon calls. He turns and leaves the room.

SCENE VII

A telephone booth at stage left. Ben is talking behind the glass.

BEN Yes. The Fairfax hotel. No. I dont know. I opened the door and there was a dead man on the bed. Yes. Room two-twelve. It's not a joke. Well call the hotel. Have the clerk check. Yes. No, I opened a wrong door.

He hangs up the telephone.

SCENE VIII

The farmhouse diningroom. Ben alone at the table with his cup of tea before him. Maven comes in in her robe. She bends and kisses him.

BEN Good night Maven.

MAVEN Are you sicklied o'er with the pale cast?

BEN What?

MAVEN *(Smiling)* Are you deep in thought?

BEN That's not what I'm deep in.

MAVEN Is it about Soldier?

BEN Yes.

She stands rubbing his shoulders.

MAVEN Do you want to tell me about it?

BEN I dont want to.

Maven sits down. Ben shakes his head. He looks at her.

BEN I lied to you. God, look at me. I didnt tell you everything.

MAVEN Tell me now.

BEN He's dead.

MAVEN *(Softly)* Oh God.

BEN I dont know what to do.

MAVEN What happened?

BEN He was dead when I got to the room.

He reaches in his sidepocket. He takes out the syringe. He takes out the spoon. The tubing.

BEN Here. Here are some of his toys. His last effects.

MAVEN Oh Ben . . .

BEN I dont know what to do, Maven.

MAVEN They'll know who he is . . . They'll . . .

BEN I took his billfold too.

MAVEN Oh Baby.

BEN When I saw him I just . . . I've never known such sadness. It was like I couldnt breathe. And then it just made me mad. I sat there in the room with him. And I just . . . I was in a rage.

MAVEN What are you going to do?

BEN I dont know.

MAVEN You cant just let them . . .

BEN Why cant I?

They sit in silence.
Maven shakes her head.

MAVEN He's still part of this family, Ben.

BEN He's dead.

MAVEN That's not good enough.

BEN So it's not good enough.

MAVEN If he's dead why cant he come home, Ben?

BEN What am I supposed to tell Carlotta?

MAVEN *(Echoing Ben's phrase)* What indeed.

BEN And Mama.

MAVEN And Mama.

BEN I cant change anything, Maven. There's nothing I can do. It wont make anything better for anybody. It will just make everything worse. A lot worse.

MAVEN You intend to take all this to the grave with you?

BEN Why not?

MAVEN I dont think you can.

BEN Alive I can manage to keep him from wrecking this family but now that he's dead I'm helpless against him?

MAVEN Something like that.

BEN God, Maven.

MAVEN I'm not going to tell you what you want to hear.

BEN I know.

MAVEN I think it's all on the line, Ben. Right here.

BEN Dont tell me that.

MAVEN You told me that principles were absolute or they werent principles. That it couldnt have to do with other people because other people change. You said there could be no exclusion clauses. That if you gave your word to someone you had to keep it even if that person were to turn against you. You had to keep it no matter what they did.

BEN I said. I said.

MAVEN Yes. You said, Ben.

BEN How am I supposed to tell her this, Maven? How?

MAVEN Dont you see what you're doing? You're getting to say, Ben. And it's not up to you. You cant know another person's torment. You of all people. Things come easy to you.

He starts to speak.

MAVEN No. They do. You cant judge, Ben. You cant get to say.

BEN I just dont think I can do it.

MAVEN Everything you worked for, Ben. It was all because you didnt think it was fair. You didnt think it was fair that people should not have what they'd worked for. You didnt think it was fair that people were left outside looking in. You didnt think it was fair that people should be singled out for dispossession or condemned to ignorance or that they should be robbed because they had no recourse or insulted because they had no rebuttal. You said there were some things that people didnt have to deserve.

You said there were some things you *couldnt* deserve. Things so sweet or so precious or even just so common to all humanity that there was no deserving them they just were given and you couldnt question them whether they fell to you or to someone else you couldnt question them. Maybe that dead boy doesnt deserve to be buried with his family. But Ben does he have to? Does he have to?

Ben looks up at her.

BEN Why are you crying? Is it because of Soldier?
MAVEN No.

He leans and takes her face in his hands and kisses her eyes.

BEN When Melissa was born I walked into the room and I was . . . I guess I was crying and I looked at you and I didnt know what to say and I said thank you. And you laughed. Do you remember?
MAVEN Yes.

He kisses her again.

BEN Let me call. Before I lose my nerve.

He rises and goes to the telephone and dials.

BEN Yes. For Louisville. Do you have the number for the police. No. It's not an emergency. Thank you.

He pushes down the receiver and dials the number.

BEN Hello. Yes. My name is Telfair and I'm calling in re-gard to . . . in regard to a man who was found dead at the Fairfax Hotel this morning. Yes. I have an identification. Yes.

He waits. He looks at Maven.

BEN Yes. Black male. Nineteen. Yes. He *was* nineteen. He was my nephew. Telfair. *His* name. Benjamin. His name was Benjamin.

SCENE IX

At stage right, the family cemetery with the stone farmhouse in the background. There are a number of stone markers and part of an iron paling fence. All the family are present and dressed in mourning and the minister is reading the service over the casket.

MINISTER Fearfulness and trembling are come upon me. And horror hath overwhelmed me. And I said, Oh that I had wings like a dove, then would I fly away and be at rest. Lo then would I wander far off. I would lodge in the wilderness. I would hast me to a shelter from the stormy wind and tempest.

A wind is blowing across the little cemetery and Carlotta who is standing next to her husband turns away and goes stage left a few steps and stands looking out away from the service. She takes off her hat and veil and shakes out her hair. Her mouth is set and her face is hard.

MINISTER Destroy, O Lord, and divide their tongue: For I have seen violence and strife in the city. Day and night they go about it upon the walls thereof. Iniquity also and mischief are in the midst of it . . . .

He breaks off and looks up.

MINISTER For it was not an enemy that reproached me. Then I could have borne it.

SCENE X

Night, the farmhouse diningroom. Ben is sitting alone with his elbows on the table and his forehead against his fists. A light comes on in the kitchen behind him and Carlotta enters the room. She comes forward and stands looking down at him. She is still dressed in black. Ben raises his head. Then he turns and looks up at her.

CARLOTTA We're leaving tomorrow. As soon as we've found a place we'll send out for the furniture and things. I'm going to let you and Mason make whatever sort of agreement he thinks is fair about the house. I'm sorry it's on your land. We cant move it.

BEN I'm sorry, Carly.

CARLOTTA I dont think you are.

BEN I know. But I am. I dont know what else to say.

He looks away. She is standing looking down at him. She shakes her head. He turns and looks at her again.

BEN What about Mama?

CARLOTTA Mama's not going anywhere.

He looks away again.

CARLOTTA Tell me one thing.

BEN Anything.

CARLOTTA Did he mean to do it?

Ben looks at her.

BEN No. I dont think he did.
CARLOTTA But I'll never know. Will I?

He looks away.

BEN No.
CARLOTTA I thought you were different, Ben.
BEN So did I.
CARLOTTA Well.

She half turns to go.

BEN I cant undo it Carly. I was wrong and I'll be sorry for it the rest of my life.
CARLOTTA So will I, Ben.

She exits.

SCENE XI

The little cemetery, stage right. It is evening and Ben is standing among the stones. The light comes on at the podium where Ben speaks.

BEN   In the fall of that year when the weather had begun to turn I thought of him more and more. I remembered his pipe. I remembered a fox we saw on the hill behind the house in the snow and I remembered small things about him. His gloves. The knees in his trousers. The way he turned the pages of his bible. I saw him here twice in the evening just at dusk and I tried small tricks to make him appear again. I'd turn my head aside and then look back quickly. Or I'd close my eyes. Or maybe it was a dream. I saw him with a great stone that he carried with much labor and I thought it was like a boundary stone and I looked for some mark or inscription on the stone but there was none. It was just a stone. Nothing is finally understood. Nothing is finally arrived at.

Grace I know is much like love and you cannot deserve it. It is freely given, without reason or equity. What could you do to deserve it? What?

I've questioned the rightness of loving that old man beyond all other souls.

What I need most is to learn charity. That most of all.

I know that small acts of valor may be all that is visible of great movements of courage within.

For we are all the elect, each one of us, and we are embarked upon a journey to something unimaginable. We do not know what will be required of us, and we have nothing to sustain us but the counsel of our fathers.

It has grown darker in the little cemetery. A wind has sprung up.

BEN Then one night when I was thinking of nothing at all he was suddenly there before me so plain I could have touched him.

Papaw materializes out of the fog upstage just at the edge of the headstones. He is naked.

BEN He came out of the darkness and at that moment everything seemed revealed to me and I could almost touch him I could almost touch his old black head and he was naked and I could see the corded muscles in his shoulders that the stone had put there and the sinews and the veins in his forearms and his small belly and his thin old man's shanks and his slender polished shins and he was so very beautiful. He was just a man, naked and alone in the universe, and he was not afraid and I wept with a joy and a sadness I'd never known and I stood there with the tears pouring down my face and he smiled at me and he held out both his hands. Hands from which all those blessings had flowed. Hands I never tired to look at. Shaped in the image of God. To make the world. To make it again and again. To make it in the very maelstrom of its undoing. Then as he began to fade I knelt in the grass and I prayed for the first time in my life. I prayed as men must have prayed ten thousand years ago to their dead kin for guidance and I knew that he would guide me all my days and that he would not fail me, not fail me, not ever fail me.

CURTAIN